ANĀGATAVAṂSA DESANĀ

The Sermon of the Chronicle-To-Be

Maitreya in royal guise.
Ruby-studded bronze from Suriyagoda Rajamahavihara, Sri Lanka
19th century

ANĀGATAVAṂSA DESANĀ

The Sermon of the Chronicle-To-Be

Translated from the Sinhala by

UDAYA MEDDEGAMA

Edited with an Indtroduction, Glossary and Notes by

JOHN CLIFORD HOLT

MOTILAL BANARSIDASS PUBLISHERS
PRIVATE LIMITED • DELHI

Reprint : Delhi, 2010
First Edition: Delhi, 1993

ISBN: 978-81-208-1133-1

MOTILAL BANARSIDASS
41 U.A. Bungalow Road, Jawahar Nagar, Delhi 110 007
8 Mahalaxmi Chamber, 22 Bhulabhai Desai Road, Mumbai 400 026
203 Royapettah High Road, Mylapore, Chennai 600 004
236, 9th Main III Block, Jayanagar, Bangalore 560 011
Sanas Plaza, 1302 Baji Rao Road, Pune 411 002
8 Camac Street, Kolkata 700 017
Ashok Rajpath, Patna 800 004
Chowk, Varanasi 221 001

Printed in India
By Jainendra Prakash Jain at Shri Jainendra Press,
A-45 Naraina, Phase-I, New Delhi 110 028
and Published by Narendra Prakash Jain for
Motilal Banarsidass Publishers Private Limited,
Bungalow Road, Delhi 110 007

To

Atulya, Indu, Achala,

Sarah, and Samuel

FOREWORD

The series editor has elsewhere pointed out that after Gautama Buddha's Parinirvāṇa, he continued as a presence in the absence, while the other two 'Jewels' (The Dharma and Saṅgha) continued in the presence. The Mahāsaṅghika sect was mainly responsible for the popular symbolic formations to fill in this presence in the absence, thus promoting the Jewel of the Buddha. One preeminent solution to this presence in the absence was the cult of the future Buddha, Maitreya, that was even accepted in the Theravāda by the Pāli name Metteyya.

The Maitreya cult has occasioned rather considerable scholarly study, and the fine text of 'references' given by John Holt does not exhaust the Western Studies since it takes no account of the French Studies.

It is a pleasure to include in the Buddhist Traditions Series this English translation from the Sinhalese of the *Anāgatavaṃsa* which is a Theravāda version for the prophecy of the future Buddha, Maitreya.

ALEX WAYMAN

CONTENTS

Foreword	vii
Preface	xi
Introduction	1
Translation of the ***Anāgatavaṃsa Desanā***	19
Glossary	57
Index	69

PREFACE

It is our hope that colleagues working in the fields of history of religions, Buddhism and South Asian studies will find this publication helpful in their research and teaching enterprises. While not a canonical text *per se*, the *Anāgatavaṃsa Desanā* is a paradigmatic example of apocalypticism and eschatology at work in the popular religious imagination.

In transliterating and editing this work from the original Sinhala, Sanskrit and Pali, we have followed the conventions of C. Carter's *Sinhala-English Dictionary*, Monier Monier-Williams' *A Sanskrit-English Dictionary*, and T.W. Rhys Davids' and William Stede's *The Pali Text Society's Pali-English Dictionary*.

We are especially grateful to Professor P.B. Meegaskumbura of the Department of Sinhala at the University of Peradeniya, Sri Lanka and to Dr. Sunil Goonasekera of the Institute of Fundamental Studies in Kandy, Sri Lanka, for their very helpful and valuable contributions and insights. We also acknowledge the support of the National Endowment of the Humanities in Washington, D.C., U.S.A., and Bowdoin College, Brunswick, Maine, U.S.A.

Regarding Professor Wayman's comment in the "Foreword", we are unaware of any significant French scholarship on the *Anāgatavaṃsa Desanā*. Our list of references was not intended as a comprehensive bibliography for "Maitreya Studies". It is only a list of works cited in the "Introduction".

UDAYA MEDDEGAMA JOHN CLIFFORD HOLT
March 18, 1992

INTRODUCTION

Throughout the historical development of Buddhist traditions in Asian cultures and societies, veneration of the *bodhisattva* Maitreya (Pāli: Metteyya, Sinhala: Maitrī; Tibetan: Byama-pa; Chinese: Mi-lo; and Japanese: Miroku) has consistently reflected eschatological visions of an ultimate spiritual salvation and, to a lesser extent, recurrent millennial dreams of collective redemption from the problematic conditions of this-worldly existence. Abiding in the splendid heavenly abode of Tuṣita in the upper strata of the Buddhist hierarchical cosmos, Maitreya is believed to be the future Buddha whose appearance in the human abode later in this world-cycle (*kalpa*) will re-establish *dharmic* norms of righteousness and provide the virtuous with an auspicious time and place to gain the final fruition of the spiritual path: *nirvāṇa*. Maitreya is thus a mythic figure symbolizing the consummate spiritual future for all Buddhists. Literally, his name means 'the friendly one.' The term *maitrī* when used in Buddhist philosophical or religious discourse, is usually taken to mean 'loving kindness', or the cultivated feeling of well-being about oneself that can be extended to all living creatures. The figure of Maitreya, therefore, embodies the spiritual hope that righteous human beings may some day live in universal concord [Abegg: 30]. As such, this belief in the coming of a future Buddha has been rightly regarded as soteriologically analogous to Judeo-Christian apocalyptic messianism, Islamic expectations of the Mahdi's return, or the re-appearance of founding culture-heroes in more traditional or 'primitive' societies. Visions of Maitreya's wondrous future age are part of the history of religions in which religieux have expressed a yearning to live amidst temporal conditions supernally conducive to the attainment of the spiritual *summum bonum.*

Historically, the cult of Maitreya has been truly pan-Asian in scope. References to this *bodhisattva* are as ancient as the *Dīgha Nikāya* of the Pāli canon and most scholars concede that his cult had penetrated the ritual life of all South Asian Buddhist communities by at least the beginning of the Christian Era. It is possible that the origins of his cult were influenced by the diffusion throughout ancient northern India of Zoroastrian soteriological beliefs concerning Šaošyant, the victorious cosmic savior figure expected to lead the forces of goodness and light to triumph over the forces of evil and darkness at the end of time [Basham: 274]. More specifically, it may be that this Iranian influence took root and was then articulated in the idea of a future buddha originally amongst Hīnayāna Buddhist Kashmiri communities several centuries following the demise of the historical Gautama Buddha [Zurcher, I: 391]. Or, it may be that the emergent belief in a future buddha owes its origins to antecedent Jain traditions regarding the continuing lineage of *tīrthaṅkaras* ('ford-makers': spiritual 'victors' exemplifying the way leading to ultimate spiritual realization), rather than to Persian Zoroastrian sources. In any case, by the time that the Lokottaravāda branch of the Mahāsaṅghikas formulated their canonical *Mahāvastu* (the earliest text in which *bodhisattvas* are conceived of as supernatural beings) Maitreya is found at the head of a list of prophesied future buddhas. Whether or not the impetus for belief in Maitreya is ultimately Persian (Zoroastrian) or Indian (Jain) in origin,

> the cult of Maitreya cannot be dated earlier than three centuries after the Buddha's nirvāṇa, and seemed to have reached its greatest influence in the period from the second to the eighth centuries A.D., the peak occurring

> about the fifth century. [Kloppenborg: 37]

Whatever the original historical genesis of the cult of Maitreya, Joseph Kitagawa has made the salient point that

> one of the most fascinating features of Maitreya is that wherever Buddhism was transplanted his figure evoked 'potential modes of creativeness' . . . in the peoples' religious apprehension and expression. [110]

In contrast to the more formal canons of the Theravāda Buddhist tradition where the cult of Maitreya seems to have occupied only a marginal place, numerous Mahāyāna *sūtras*, such as the *Saddharmapuṇḍarīka* (*Lotus of the True Law*) and the *Vajracchedikā* (*Diamond Sūtra*) afford Maitreya a very prominent salvific role along with *bodhisattvas* Avalokiteśvara, Mañjuśrī and Amitābha. To be reborn in the age of Maitreya was regarded as an especially auspicious penultimate spiritual fate. In India, it is likely that visions of Maitreya's future age contributed significantly to the emerging belief in Amitābha's paradise, Sukhāvatī (the 'Pure Land'), which, when transplanted to China and Japan, eventually became the cornerstone of the most widespread sectarian Buddhist tradition appealing to the laity of East Asia.

The desire to dwell in the presence of Maitreya, however, was not limited to pious laity. Many Buddhist monks of various Mahāyāna Buddhist schools flourishing in China are known to have engaged in elaborate practices of meditation hoping to ascend to the Tuṣita heaven to share in Mi-lo's spiritual resplendence; it is likely that the meditational states they experienced were correlated to a projective metaphysical experience of the Tuṣita abode. Others, influenced perhaps by Taoist practices to promote longevity or immortality, aspired to prolong their temporal lives until Mi-lo's expected descent into this world. Periodically in China, the cult of Mi-lo also inspired sectarian and revolutionary political movements from the time of the Sui dynasty through the Ming and Manchu. In these contexts, the expected descent of Mi-lo represented popular aspirations for the disestablishment of an oppressive social, economic and political status quo and the inauguration of a new age wherein access to power and material wealth would be more egalitarian. On the other hand, the eighth century T'ang dynasty Empress Wu claimed to be an incarnation of Mi-lo [Chen: 428] thus legitimating her position at the apex of hierarchy.

In traditional Korea, the cult of Mi-ruk (Maitreya) was particularly significant in creating a religiously based nationalism, especially among the Hwa-rang Do, aristocratic youths who believed that Maitreya protected and promoted their interests in unifying the Korean state. [Kitagawa: 119]

Veneration of Miroku has also been associated with monastic and popular Buddhism since the religion's introduction into Japanese society under Prince Shōtoku (7th century A.D.) and has become a primary article of inspired faith especially within a number of the so-called 'new religious movements' of the past century. From the twelfth century to the present in popular Japanese culture, Miroku also has been known as the obese and almost silly, comic figure of Japanese sculpture symbolizing good luck or an optimistic view of the future, one filled with great satisfaction for those who live the good religious life in the present.

Throughout the history of Mahāyāna in East Asia, the twin motifs of personal *ascent* to Maitreya's abode by means of individually realized esoteric spiritual pursuits and the *descent* of Maitreya to this human world in times of collective existential distress respectively embodied the eschatological hopes of religious consummation. The former was a matter of personal soteriological aspiration while the latter a collective hope socially engendered.

The importance of Maitreya in Theravāda Buddhism has

never been a conspicuous element in canonical sources. Despite its pretensions, the *Anāgatavaṃsa* was never accorded canonical status. Its decidedly popular religious imagery was thoroughly the stuff of lay Theravāda piety and was conveniently appropriated by Buddhist royalty to legitimate kingship. In fact, the original elaborated Sinhala version of the *Anāgatavaṃsa*, the text from which our present translated recension descends, was compiled by Parākramabāhu Mahāthera of Vilgammula at the request of Parākramabāhu IV of Kurunegala [1303-33 A.D.] because it 'was one which the king enjoyed listening to during nights when sermons were delivered' [Godakumbura: 102]. When the close relationship between belief in Metteyya and the role of the universal monarch (*cakkavatti*) is known, it is clear why this text was especially appealing to Buddhist kings.

The only Theravāda Pāli canonical reference to Metteyya is found in the mythic *Cakkavatti-sīhanāda-suttanta* of the *Suttapiṭaka's Dialogues of the Buddha*. In this text, the coming of Metteyya is referred to only after a thoroughgoing description of the reestablishment of moral righteousness throughout the cosmos by a universal monarch following a long period of decline in the quality of temporal existence owing to a growing human propensity for evil conduct. The *cakkavatti* heralds the advent of Metteyya by conquering the human world through a morally righteous *dharm*ic conquest, rather than gaining victorious rule by brute military might. His *dharma* is the *pañcaśīla*: the five-fold moral norm—abstaining from taking like, stealing, lying, lust and intoxication. He is the royal religious layman *par excellence* living and ruling according to the principles of altruism. The excellence of his own behavior is matched only by the splendid living conditions he provides for those living under his dominion. Indeed, the latter is a consequence of the former. It has been suggested that this mythic model of righteous kingship based on *dharma* rather than *daṇḍa* (military might) 'served to stimulate King Aśoka's [third century B.C.] efforts in articulating *dharma* as the religiously inspired social and political principle of justice and morality' [Kitagawa: 110]. In turn, Aśoka's legacy of a 'practical *dharma*' became an intrinsic factor in the development of subsequent paradigms of Theravāda Buddhist kingship. According to the *Anāgatavaṃsa Desanā*, Aśoka will eventually be reborn in the age of Metteyya and become one of his two chief monastic disciples.

Specific identifications between kingship and Metteyya were especially rich in the Theravāda Pāli and Sinhala traditional accounts of exemplary political rule in ancient and medieval Sri Lanka. In the *Mahāvaṃsa's* account of the great Sinhalese warrior king Duṭṭhāgamaṇī who united Lanka 'under one umbrella' by defeating the great Tamil king Elāra, the prediction is made that this national hero will ultimately be reborn into the family of Metteyya [XXXII: 83]. While Duṭṭhagamaṇī's conquest is accomplished by might rather than by moral suasion, his association with Metteyya is legitimated in the *Mahāvaṃsa's* Theravāda monastic perspective because of his leadership in assuring the future of the Buddha's religion. The association between kingship and the future buddha eventually becomes so entwined in Sinhala tradition that by the fifth century A.D., the Anurādhāpura king Dhātusena commissioned a statue of Metteyya sculpted in his own likeness 'with the complete equipment of a king' [*Cūḷavaṃsa* XXXVIII: 68]. There is a good deal more literary and artistic evidence to suggest that the bodhisattva ideal was often fully appropriated by Sinhalese kings who aspired to become buddhas themselves.

There is little question that the Sinhalese conception of kingship was affected by Mahāyāna conceptions of the bodhisattva. Indeed, the claims by kings to be bodhisattvas either directly or indirectly follow shortly after the historical introduction and subsequent suppression of Mahāyāna on the island. Royal attraction to the *bodhisattva* ideal seems to have been something of the following appeal: just as the *bodhisattva* works tirelessly out of selfless compassion for the ultimate spiritual well-being of his devotees, so the king should expend his efforts to seek better conditions of well-being for his subjects. But since Metteyya is the only *bodhisattva* and future buddha formally recognized by Theravāda tradition, and since Theravāda eventually emerged in Sri Lanka as the sole religious object of royal patronage, the implication is that many later kings, in regarding themselves as *bodhisattvas*, were simultaneously making the claim to be 'Metteyya-in-the-making'. In the tenth century inscriptions of Mahinda IV, we find the statement that only *bodhisattvas* might become kings of Lanka [*Epigraphia Zeylanica* 1: 240] and by this time the Theravāda claim to legitimacy had for centuries been secured. In part, the conflation of the *cakkavatti* model of kingship with royal aspirations to become the Buddha Metteyya symbolizes a political domestication of the cult of Maitreya which, to a certain extent, resulted in the partial submergence of the public devotional cult of the *bodhisattva per se* apart from its associations with kingship.

It is interesting to note, however, that the Sinhala political cult of Maitreya did not re-surface as a millennial movement in Sri Lanka following the disestablishment of kingship by the British in 1815, a phenomenon which repeatedly occurred during the colonial and post-colonial phases of Burmese history [Sarkisyanz: 149-65] after the British deposed the last Burmese king in the 1880s. As late as the 1950s and early 1960s, Burmese Prime Minister U Nu was regarded by many traditional folk as a buddha-in-the-making attempting to establish a this-worldly *nirvāṇa* through the creation of a perfect society [Sarkisyanz: 210-28]. But by this time in the history of Sri Lankan Buddhism, Maitreya's identity had undergone yet further transformations through his association with other dominant religious motifs. The historian looks in vain for Maitreya-inspired millennial movements during the colonial era of Sri Lankan history similar in character to the events and claims being made in Burma.

The domestication of the cult of Maitreya into the political fabric of traditional Theravāda societies did not exhaust the religious significance of Maitreya veneration. Indeed, sculptures and paintings of Maitreya can be found in many Sinhala Theravāda monasteries today, and these bear no resemblance to royalty. To the contrary, they have been molded or painted to conform to the iconography of buddha figures. Over the course of time, a distinctive iconographic tradition was attached to Maitreya figures. The most pronounced feature of Maitreya sculptures in Sri Lanka was the *stūpa* worn as a crown. In temple paintings, Maitreya was usually depicted in Tuṣita heaven preaching the *buddhadharma* to an attentive divine audience. There is little here to suggest a conflation with kingship in these traditions of artistic representation; instead, they suggest a continued veneration for the future figure who would once again re-establish *dharma*.

Metteyya is rarely mentioned in the traditional commentaries and chronicles of the Sinhalese Theravādins. But one significant reference occurs in connection with the great orthodox commentator Buddhaghosa whose works became normative interpretations of the spiritual path for the Theravāda monastic community. According to this account, after mischievous *devatās* (minor deities) had caused his *magnum opus*, the *Visuddhimagga* ('The Path of Purity') to disappear twice, Buddhaghosa reproduced the text a third time from memory without an error. The response of the *bhikkhu* witnesses to this 'miracle' of memory and erudition was: 'without doubt, this must be Metteyya' [*Cūḷavaṃsa* XXXVII: 242]. What this story and the previously mentioned artistic traditions seem to suggest is that not only did Maitreya come to be associated with visions of perfected kingship, but he also seems to have been continuously associated with the ideal of the perfected monk.

Not only has Maitreya been identified with the perfections of kingship and monasticism, but in traditional Sinhala Buddhist culture since late medieval times, he is also associated with Nātha Deviyo, the highest of the four national guardian deities in the Sinhala pantheon as it is conceived by traditional upcountry Kandyan village Sinhalese. Before the late medieval period, Nātha was not included in the cult of national guardian deities. But Nātha, whose original identity is the Mahāyāna *bodhisattva* Avalokiteśvara, became the patron deity and legitimator of Kandyan kings in the late medieval period. His temple is located directly opposite the Daḷadā Māligāva (Temple of the Buddha's Tooth Relic) in the last of the traditional capital cities of the Sinhalese. It is here that kings were given their formal names. Earlier medieval inscriptions attest to Nātha's perceived efficacy in protecting the kingdom and its religion from external threats [*Epigraphia Zeylanica* 4: 310-11]. Like the other national guardian deities of Sri Lanka in late Kandyan cosmology (Viṣṇu, Kataragama or Skanda, and Pattinī), Nātha is not just a deity, but is also regarded as a *bodhisattva*. The perception that he is the highest of the gods and therefore the most advanced in his quest for buddhahood was confirmed, if not established, in the late 18th century by King Kīrti Śrī Rājasiṃha when the processional order of the annual Äsaḷa Perahära pageant was re-organized. The procession was and remains at once a symbolic ritual statement defining the structure of traditional Sinhala society as well as the hierarchy of the Buddhist pantheon [Seneviratne: 108-14]. Nātha's retinue is positioned immediately following the representatives of the Daḷadā Māligāva (symbolic of the Buddha's presence) thus confirming the perception that Nātha is next in line to become a buddha. The implication, then, at least from the Theravāda point of view, is that Nātha is to become Maitreya. Because Nātha is so close to becoming a buddha, he is seen as not only the highest of the deities, but also the most distant and therefore the least likely to respond to the needs of those who call upon him for assistance in this-worldly affairs. This particular belief, that Nātha is Maitreya, is the most common aspect of Maitreya veneration in modern Sri Lanka. While it is not at all emphasized by learned monks or the educated lay elite, it is a matter of fact to villagers in the rural highlands of traditional Sri Lanka.

In all of these associations (royal, monastic, and divine), a consistent motif is expressed: the image of a perfected existence to be realized again in the future. This theme is, in fact, the central expression of the *Anāgatavaṃsa Desanā* ('The Sermon of the Chronicle-to-be') and at the heart of traditional lay Buddhist aspirations.

The *Anāgatavaṃsa Desanā* is sometimes a ritual text. That is, it is occasionally read by *bhikkhus* to the laity within the context of liturgical observances, especially *poya* (full-moon day) ceremonies conducted for the laity each month by monks at Buddhist *vihāras*. The text we have translated from the Sinhala, which seems to date from the 18th century (on the basis of the language employed), is itself a shorter version of the elaborate and elegant Sinhala *Anāgatavaṃsa* composed by Vilgammula in the fourteenth century which, in turn, is ultimately based on the 142 verse original Pāli poem [See Minayeff: 33ff]. Some of the original Pāli verses have been preserved in the surviving narrative lending authority to the text for its lay audience. It purports to be *buddhavacana* ('words of the Buddha'). But such a claim is immediately betrayed by its frequent shifts in voice, which indicate a history of materials from various sources being inserted, along with third person references to the Buddha Gotama (its purported author) within the narrative itself. There are also several redundancies with regard to specifying who will be the chief disciples under Maitreya in the future order of monks. The sermon is heavily didactic in nature ending with prescriptive behavioral injunctions of the type which belie a monastic expediency not uncommonly found in sermonic literature of this genre. Its decidedly popular character is also attested by its mixture of Sanskrit and Pāli words within the Sinhala narrative. Further, while all names of a place in the text refer to Indian locales in keeping with the original *Anāgatavaṃsa* poem, there are frequent allusions to flora which are found only in Sri Lanka. But since the *Anāgatavaṃsa* is referred to in Buddhagosa's fifth century A.D. *Visuddhimagga*, the original text must be of ancient origins. In any event, our recension clearly has a history of being recast several times. Indeed, very similar sections of our text can be found in other examples of popular medieval Sinhala literature including the *Ratnavaliya* and the *Pujavaliya*. The intended audience is the mass of traditional lay Buddhists who observe *aṭṭha sīla* (the 'eight-fold morality') on full-moon days and are eager to hear inspired sermons about the eventual *karm*ic rewards of their efforts. For them, *nirvāṇa* is a far too distant goal to hope for in the present. But eventual rebirth in Maitreya's time is not out of the question at all.

The *Anāgatavaṃsa Desanā* articulates a number of themes common to popular Buddhist conceptions of buddhahood, society and cosmos. Cosmologically, the future kingdom of Ketumatī in which Maitreya will prosper is positioned in the centre of the world in the traditionally conceived *maṇḍala*-shaped flat disc cosmos. Ketumatī corresponds to the notion of the earthly 'sacred city', an idea perpetuated by ruling monarchs throughout South and Southeast Asia to enhance the aura of sanctity which they wished to promulgate amongst their subjects. The symbolism employed to describe the phantasmagoric palace of King Saṅka, the *cakkavatti* ruling over Ketumatī in the age of Maitreya, is also drawn from traditional Buddhist cosmography. The seven walls surrounding the palace are architectural references to the seven concentric mountain ranges surrounding Mt. Meru which itself is symbolized by the fantastic royal palace. Mt. Meru, as the pivot of the cosmos located in the centre of Jambūdvīpa (the abode of humankind) is the veritable *axis mundi* of the universe. Such imagery was historically incorporated by Buddhist kings in Burma and Thailand in the construction of their own palaces to reinforce the perception that the king was an 'embryo-buddha' or the this-worldly counterpart to the 'king of gods'.

The vision of societal conditions in the *Anāgatavaṃsa's* Ketumatī is similarly phantasmagoric. They would seem to reflect all of the wonders of the villagers' imagination of heavenly existence heaped one on top of each other and constitute a direct antithesis to the life-style of the ascetic. It is a magnificent vision of temporal existence. No one will want for anything in the kingdom of Ketumatī. *Kalpa vṛkṣa*s, or wishing trees, will provide any material amenity for the asking. Hence, there will be no conditions for craving and no poverty and therefore no theft, lying, killing or other demeritorious forms of behavior. There will be no pollution of any kind. Birds will not perch on the branches of Maitreya's bodhi tree and when humans defecate or urinate, pits will appear and subsequently turn into lotus ponds. Thus, there will be nothing foul in this perfumed paradise. Since rice will grow magically, there will be no work of cultivation and no famine. All physical human conditions will be ideal. The span of human life will be almost without limit. There will be no religious sectarianism of any sort. Even the giving of alms to the *Saṅgha* will be miraculously accomplished by means of air-born *vihāra*s (monasteries) and *gandhakuṭī*s (dwelling chambers of the Buddha) which will be magically transported with monks and Maitreya to the houses (all of which will be constructed out of precious stones) of the laity. In short, the conditions of life in Ketumatī will be so ideal that none of the psychological propensities leading to attachment and ego-grasping will arise. This brings us to the doctrinal heart of the matter.

The career of Maitreya in the future Ketumatī is remarkable only in terms of the splendid conditions within which he and his followers will dwell. His 'biography' essentially follows the well-known events of the biography of the historical Gotama Buddha: his birth, the story of the 'four signs', his renunciation, his enlightenment, his first sermon, etc. While his body is massive in size, like Gotama's it possesses the thirty-two marks of a *mahāpuruṣa,* a 'great man' destined to become either a buddha or a *cakkavatti.* But substantively, there is nothing unique in the biography of Maitreya which differs significantly in any way from Gotama's career. What is different, of course, are the wonders of this perfumed existence into which Maitreya is reborn and into which the virtuous may also aspire as the result of merit-makings and moralities realized in previous existences.

If there is a drama illustrating doctrine in the *Anāgatavaṃsa Desanā* which can be taken allegorically for every man, it is concerned with the transformations of the humble low caste basket-weaver and his son whose remarkable rebirths as a great king and the *cakkavatti* Saṅkha are the direct result of *karm*ic retribution stemming from their building a simple abode for the dwelling of Buddhist monks. What the story illustrates is the potential salvific power deriving from actions of selfless-giving to worthy recipients, i.e. the *saṅgha,* who are resolutely pursuing the ultimate goal of *nirvāṇa* by means of disciplined self-effort. The point here, which could be construed cynically as a monastic attempt to coerce the laity into unqualified material support, is that providing amenities to assist those aiming for the ultimate spiritual goal leads to one's own spiritual attainment as well. Indeed, this is the religious significance of *karma*—that actions undertaken without regard to self, but instead in the interest of others, is what leads to the realization of one's own spiritual goal. This is not the means to salvation through meditation or through illuminative knowledge, but the means to salvation through *action.* As such, it is thoroughly a lay Buddhist ethic.

Wishing and waiting to be reborn in Maitreya's age has long been a common aspiration for traditional lay Buddhists. In the Kandyan region of Sri Lanka, at least one fifteenth century inscription has been found articulating this particular religious hope. It is, however, at variance with canonical understandings of how the path to *nirvāṇa* is ultimately attained. As such, veneration of Maitreya and the hope to be reborn in his age is not very current within circles of 'Buddhist modernists', educated Buddhists who seek to return to the original message of the Buddha and eschew those features of the religion which they perceive as cultural and social accretions [Southwold: 202-13 and Bechert, *passim*].

Since the early decades of the twentieth century in Buddhist Sri Lanka, the Theravāda community has experienced a significant reform as the result of the promulgation of 'pure doctrine' by the *saṅgha* and educated Buddhist laity. To be sure, this is also partially the result of the proliferation of canonical texts now available in printed form for the inquiring reader. But it is also the result of the 'monasticization' of the laity, the process by which many aspects of traditional monastic spiritual life, primarily meditation, have been taken up and cultivated in earnest by the laity. The consequences of this process for the laity has been prodigious, especially in urban centers of the country where competition between Buddhism and Christianity amongst educated laity was at one time quite pronounced. One of the facets of this process has to do with the conception of *nirvāṇa* and the path to be followed towards its attainment by the layman.

In traditional lay circles, *nirvāṇa* has been regarded as an ever distant goal rarely attained by even the most spiritually advanced monks. Part of the reason for this view of *nirvāṇa* lies in traditional conceptions of time. The life-time of a buddha is regarded as particularly auspicious, as *dharma* is clearly articulated and the master-teacher is present to exemplify the spiritual path. But as time passes, and followers of *dharma* become ever more removed from the lifetime of a buddha, the power of *dharma* declines and conditions for its realization become increasingly difficult. Perhaps the clearest expression of this scenario has been articulated in the Mahāyāna Japanese Pure Land schools which speak of the present and last age of this world-cycle as *mappo*, the current age of degeneracy wherein spiritual progress can only be attained through acts of faith rather than merit. The doctrine of the declining power of *dharma*, however, was articulated early on in the history of Indian Mahāyāna in the *Lotus Sūtra* and it was also assumed within the canonical and popular traditions of Theravāda as well. Essentially, it holds that the quality of human existence, and hence the capability of adhering to the spiritual path leading to *nirvāṇa*, decreases until the appearance of another buddha. For Theravāda, this buddha is Maitreya and rebirth during his time is regarded as the result of performing fortuitous *karm*ic acts in the present. Herein, the Theravāda lay ideology of salvation differs from that of the Japanese Pure Land schools. *Karma* continues to count heavily on an individual basis. Rebirth in Maitreya's age is not just a matter of faith. This, then, becomes the soteriological rationale for virtuous behavior: on the basis of meritorious and moral actions eventual rebirth during the age of Maitreya when conditions will be such that attainment of *nirvāṇa* will once again become a spiritual goal within reach.

This notion, as we have said, seems to be at odds with the ethos of 'Buddhist modernism' wherein *nirvāṇa* is understood to be a thoroughly reachable goal for anyone, monk or layman, who masters the spiritual path. Moreover, it is a notion that has recently been fundamentally criticized by zealous advocates of this '*nirvāṇa*-here-and-now' school. For them, hoping for rebirth in Maitreya's auspicious age dodges and delays facing the compelling and immediate need to get down to the serious disciplined spiritual quest which everyone eventually will need to complete. Like Marxist ideologues critiquing the narcotic affect of 'pie-in-the-sky' religion, they argue: why put off to the future that which ought to be accomplished now? In their perspective, Maitreya is of value only as a symbol, a symbol of the future life which can be realized if and when all people make genuine spiritual progress (along the lines which they advocate). In other words, the quality of the future is dependent upon religious acts in the present.

As a matter of fact, traditional village Buddhists would have no problems with these very principles. The difference between them and 'modern Buddhists' lies in exactly what constitutes the appropriate spiritual actions in the present age. The *Anāgatavaṃsa Desanā* concludes with a litany of actions incumbent upon all Buddhists which will determine who will see Maitreya and who will not. These actions continue to correspond to traditional lay understandings and continue to form the heart of the lay Buddhist religious ethos in village settings. They are divided into two main groups: (1) those concerned with the practical material support of the monastic *saṅgha* and its mission to make known the teachings of the Buddha, and (2) those of a devotional and moral nature. Many of the same actions are advocated in commentaries to the *Jātakas*, the *Mahāvaṃsa*, the *Visuddhimagga*, and the *Dhamma-saṅgaṇi* [Kloppenborg: 42-44], all monastic sources. They are clearly rooted in the ideology of merit rather than in the ideology of the modern Buddhistic '*nirvāṇa*-here-and-now'.

As it stands and as it is used, the *Anāgatavaṃsa Desanā* remains a thoroughly popular text. For those westerners whose view of Buddhism is the product of a more philosophical approach, it is a helpful reminder that for the past 2,500 years, Buddhism has been a religion that has thoroughly blended with the mythic imagination of South Asian peoples and cultures; and, that it has been embraced as a world view and sustained as a tradition by the common folk in far greater numbers than its esteemed virtuosos. But whether or not it will continue in its more popular forms far into the future is an open question as Asian societies and cultures experience the rapid process of modernization. Ironically, this raises a very interesting question regarding the continued future and religious efficacy of 'the Sermon of the Chronicle-to-be'.

REFERENCES

Abegg, E. 'Der Buddha Maitreya.' *Mitteilungen der Schweizerischen Gesellschaft dee Freunde ostasiatischer Kultur* 7, 1945.

Basham, A. L. *The Wonder That Was India.* New York: Grove Press, 1954.

Bechert, Heinz. *Buddhismus, Staat und Gesellschaft in den Landerns Theravada Buddhismus.* 2 vols. Frankfurt am Main: Metzer, 1966.

Chen, Kenneth. *Buddhism in China.* Princeton, NJ: Princeton University Press, 1964.

Epigraphia Zeylanica. 5 vols. (to date). London: Oxford University Press, 1904-.

Godakumbura, C.E. *Sinhalese Literature.* Colombo: Colombo Apothecaries Co., 1955.

Hardacre, Helen, and Sponberg, Alan. *Maitreya: The Future Buddha.* New York: Cambridge University Press, 1988.

Kitagawa, Joseph M. 'The Career of Maitreya, with Special Reference to Japan.' *History of Religions* 21 (1981).

Kloppenborg, Ria. 'The Place of Maitreya in Early and Theravada Buddhism and the Conditions fór Rebirth in his Time.' *Proceedings of the 30th International Conference of Human Sciences in Asia and North Africa,* 1976. Mexico City: El Colegio de Mexico, 1982.

Mahāvaṃsa (The Great Chronicle of Ceylon). Trans. by Wilhelm Geiger. London: for the Pāli Text Society by Luzac and Co., 1912.

Minayeff, J. 'The Anāgatavaṃsa.' *Journal of the Pāli Text Society.* 1886.

Sarkisyanz, E. *Buddhist Backgrounds of the Burmese Revolution.* The Hague: Martinis Nijhoff, 1965.

Seneviratne, H.L. *Rituals of the Kandyan State.* Cambridge, UK: Cambridge University Press, 1978.

Southwold, Martin. *Buddhism in Life: The Anthropological Study of Religion and the Practise of Sinhalese Buddhism.* Manchester, UK: Manchester University Press, 1983.

TRANSLATION
OF THE
ANĀGATAVAṂSA DESANĀ

Sāriputta Invites the Buddha Gotama to Preach

Our great *bodhisattva*,[1] the benefactor of the whole world, having successfully completed all the *pāramitās*, departing from life in *Tuṣitapura* heaven, being conceived in the womb of Queen Mahāmāyā with King Śuddhodana as his father in the kingdom of Kimbulvat, coming forth from the womb of the queen, growing up gradually as the moon grows full, having lived in incomparable regal splendor and glory for twenty-nine years in the royal palace, discarding the heritage of the *cakravartin* he was to become within a week's time, conquering all *māras* under the *bodhi* tree, attaining great buddhahood, making five types of *bhikkhus* and innumerable divine beings drunk with the nectar called *nirvāṇa*, while residing at the Veḷuvana monastery at the invitation of King Bimbisāra, visited the city of Kiṁbulvat accompanied by twenty *theras* and *arhant bhikkhus* at the behest of his father King Śuddhodana and rose from his seat into the sky in order to perform the unique and incomparable miracle called *yamaka pratihārya* for the purpose of vanquishing the pride of thousands of his relatives who would not bow down before him.

On that occasion, at the request of arhant Sāriputta,[2] he preached the *Buddhavaṃsa*, which is included in the *Cariyāpiṭaka*, and thus an *asaṃkhyā* of deities reached the golden fruit of the spiritual path, another *asaṃkhyā* of deities

1. All italicized words are defined and elaborated in the glossary.
2. Sāriputta and Moggallāna are the two chief disciples of Gotama Buddha. Both are frequently portrayed in Buddhist art standing or sitting to the right and left of the Buddha respectively. Sāriputta was known for his penetrating understanding of the Buddha's *dharma* and Moggallāna for his knowledge of supramundane power. Thus, Sāriputta is often associated with texts claiming to explicate the true teaching.

reached within one life-time of its final attainment, and millions of *brahmās* gained *nirvāṇa*.

Then Thera Sāriputta, the captain of the *dharma*, seeing that the gods' longing for *dharma* had not been satiated, dressing himself with his robe so as to cover one shoulder, approaching Lord Buddha in the manner in which an eldest son would approach a *cakravartin,* bowing down respectfully keeping his two hands touching his head, said:

> My master Lord Buddha, after listening to this special *dharma*-talk of yours, all doubts of mine and others have disappeared. Further, you have said that in this same *kalpa* another Buddha called Maitreya[3] will be born and how glorious his reign will be.

And so Sāriputta asked him to preach once again. Having been so requested, Lord Buddha began the sermon of the *Anāgatavaṃsa* as one rain falls on top of another.

---

3. In Sinhala, Maitreya's name is spelled in a number of ways including 'Meithreya', 'Maithri, and 'Mete'; in Pāli, the name is given as 'Metteyya' and in Sanskrit as 'Maitreya'. All these terms are derived from the Sanskrit term *mitra* meaning 'friend' or companion. In the *Ṛg Veda*, *Mitra* is extolled as a deity who calls men to action in order to sustain the earth and the sky. The term is consistently used in Sanskrit compounds to mean 'friendly'. The Pāli term *mettā* refers to the cultivation of love or amity towards onself and others and is one of the perfections to be attained on the path of the bodhisattva; the Pāli verb *mid* can also mean 'to fatten' which provides a clue to the impetus for the manner in which Maitreya is fashioned in the sculptural traditions of Chinese and Japanese Mahāyāna as a jolly and obese, care-free future buddha. In sum, the bodhisattva Maitreya may be taken as a mythic personification of the virtue of 'loving kindness'. However, in popular Sinhala tradition dating back to the nineteenth century, Nātha (originally Avalokiteśvara but later transformed into one of the four guardian deities of Kandyan cosmology) is identified as Maitrī-in-the-making.

The Great Prophecy

The future Buddha Maitreya, passing through *saṃsāra* in countless births and deaths as the result of various actions, associating with good companions [only] such as buddhas, *pratyekabuddhas*, and *āryaśrāvakas*, living only in appropriate regions through a hundred thousand *koṭis* of births, fulfilling the four-fold pleasures such as associating with just people, having the presence of mind to listen to *dharma*, living according to the principle of *dharma*, sixteen *asaṃkhyā kalpas* before this present time became a *cakravartin* by the name of Prabhavanta in *Madhya Maṇḍala* of *Jambūdvīpa* and possessed the seven jewels and four noble miraculous powers;[4] while touring over the four great islands[5] situated around Mt. Meru, he made all people observe *pañlaśīla* and governed his *cakravartin* kingdom like the king of gods in the company of gods. At that time, there was an omniscient buddha named Muhurta who pleased the people with his preaching of the good *dharma* and, having a hundred thousand millions of followers, went through villages, towns, cities and kingdoms to please and save the people of the world. Then the *cakravartin*

---

4. Here 'seven types of gems' (*sapta ratna*) refers to the presence and possessions of a universal monarch: his cart, elephant, horse, queen, minister, eldest son, and the gem which produces whatever he desires. In later parts of the text, it literally refers to materials by which fabulous palaces are made. The 'four noble miraculous powers' (*ṛddhi*) are attained in higher states of meditation enabling the meditator to perform superhuman feats. Together, these two phrases emphasize the total power of the *cakravartin* as he prepares the cosmos for the appearance of a buddha.
5. In traditional Buddhist cosmography, the world is divided into four continents or islands which surround the cosmic mountain Mahāmeru: Uttarakuru (north), Pūrvavideṣa (East), Aparagodāna (West) and Jambūdvīpa (South). The latter is the abode of men where buddhas may be born. It is the *dharma* of a *cakravartin* to tour all the continents in making a peaceful conquest.

Prabhavanta, who is the bodhisattva Maitreya, having heard about the birth of the Buddha, proceeded to visit him in the company of a great multitude of people covering an area of thirty *yojanas*. Having thus come to visit the Buddha, offering him various gems, kneeling before him with reverence and love as if diving into a stream of nectar, sitting up and being enthralled with the happiness that comes from meeting a buddha, sat at a suitable distance with his followers, and having heard the pleasing *dharma* preached in the sweet voice which has eight qualities, having then attained an extremely pleasing mindset, renouncing his kingdom with its seven types of jewels and great wealth, became a *bhikkhu* known as Ratna Sthavira in the order of that buddha—who shines like the full moon in the sky-like *sāsana*, developing such qualities as *śīla* and *samādhi* to gain the five-fold *abhijñā* and the eight-fold *samāpatti* cultivated in *dhyāna*. In living through that birth, he had the fortitude and power to become an arhant; still, he did not achieve that because of his magnanimous kindness to all the people still suffering in *saṃsāra* wishing for buddhahood. On that day, having the eight-fold *samodhāna dharma*, *madhyama śraddhā* and, especially the desire for *dāna* by donating his own life, he made continuous efforts at giving of himself.

Bhikkhus assembled in the hall of *dharma* began a discussion of the following nature: Will this *bhikkhu* bent on giving be born as *Śakra*, the king of gods, or as *Mahā Brahmā*, or as *Māra*? Or will he become a buddha?

At that time, the buddha named Muhūrta, seated on the especially decorated buddha-seat, just like the young sun with thousands of rays rising over the *Udaya Parvata* making the entire ocean shine, a halo emanating out of his body illuminating completely the hall of *dharma* sermons, focused his two eyes on the *bhikkhus* surrounding him like a pair of bees travelling through a full bloomed pond of red lotuses, and knowing all their thoughts, opened his mouth like a box full of four perfumes, pleased the *bhikkhus* with his utterance which was like the voice of Brahmā with its eight qualities:

> O *bhikkhus*, this *bhikkhu* Ratna is not an ordinary person; he is a future buddha; at the end of sixteen *kalpas*, he will become a great buddha like myself by the name of Maitreya.
>
> In the future birth when he attains buddhahood, he will live in a kingdom named Ketumatī ruled over by a *cakravartin* named Sankha. His father will be a brahman named Subrāhmaṇa who will be a chief counsellor to that king. A brahman woman named Brahmawathie will be his mother. Aśoka and Brahmadeva will be his chief disciples. The name of his attending disciple will be Siṃha. His two chief female disciples will be Padumā and Sumanā and his two chief lay disciples will be Sudhāna and Saṅgha. His two chief female lay attendants will be Yasavathie and Saṅghā. His *bodhi* [tree] will be the *nā* tree. His buddha-body will be eighty-eight *riyan* in height, his halo will spread over an area of twenty-five yojanas, and his lifespan will be eighty thousand years.

Having proclaimed this prophecy and having thanked his listeners, the Buddha got up from his seat and went into his *gandhakuṭī*.

The Resolution

Thereafter, this great and noble person [Maitreya], whose mind was filled with pleasure and who was venerated by men and gods, began to examine the means to attain buddhahood: *dāna*, *sīla*, *nekkhamma*, *paññā*, *viriya*, *khanti*, *sacca*, *adhiṭṭhāna*, *mettā* and *upekkhā*. He meditated over these ten perfections in ascending and descending orders. Then he caused all the mountains in the ten thousand universes such as Mahāmeru and Yugandhara to tremble and he realized that there were no other perfections except these ten. He observed them with determination and from that moment on was never born into any of the eighteen unbefitting places such as the Avīci hell. Through sixteen *asaṃkhyā kalpa*s he fulfilled the ten perfections with increasing courage. Since before our Lord Gotama Buddha became enlightened, he was reborn into the Tuṣitapura heaven preaching *dharma* to gods. He still lives in Tuṣitapura heaven with his followers.

And when shall he become the Buddha? The *karuṇasāsana* will last for five thousand years after which, as the result of a dominance of demerit, the maximum age of a human being will gradually deteriorate to ten years. At that time, people will be similar to animals. They will not observe the difference between themselves and their parents, nor will they observe a difference between a sister or a sister-in-law, a brother or a nephew or even one's own daughter. They will only love themselves. Five month old boys will marry five month old girls. All the tastes will disappear. Rice cooked with inferior grains will be considered fit for kings. The world will be devoid of all luxuries and will be destroyed in the *kalpa* called Sattāntara as a result of an abundance of hatred in the minds of the people.

The Destruction of the Old World and the Beginning of the New

Seven days before the destruction of that *kalpa*, some *kāmāvacara* deities dressed as if bereaving, will go all over this human world and warn [the people]:

> O men, seven days from today, a dangerous and destructive rain called the *mṛgasaṃvarṣa* will fall for seven days, and those who get wet will perceive each other as game

and try to kill each other. Those hoping to save themselves must collect provisions such as rice, salt, firewood and repair protective places like caves.

The deities will travel through a hundred million universes. On hearing this [warning], people, being naturally foolish, will laugh, saying: 'Who has ever seen or heard of such a thing? What nonsense!' But some wise men will say: 'Who knows what could happen? We shall abide by the words of these gods.' And these people will live in caves and other hiding places so as not to see one another.

Then the *mṛgasaṃvarṣa* will begin to fall heavily all over the hundred million universes. Those who get wet with even one drop of that rain will seem like game to one another. 'Hey, run, shoot that deer, kill it!' And so they will chase each other. Blades of grass and leaves will turn into sharp swords. During those seven days, people will turn this world into one big heap of meat and the ocean will be filled with the blood of those killing one another. When the rain ceases after seven days, those who are still living will come out of their hiding places and see the mutilated parts of their relations' bodies—their hands, feet, ears, and noses. Being overcome by grief and compassion, they will say: 'Our relatives killed themselves by not listening to us. Now, all of us who remain will give up killing from today.' So, these survivors will desist from killing and from that meritorious action, their children will live for twenty years. By desisting from stealing, their children will live for thirty years. By giving up adultery, their children will live for forty years. Giving up lying, the children they beget will live for fifty years. Giving up gossip, their children will live for sixty years and abstain from the ten-fold acts of demerit. Simultaneously, they will observe the ten acts of merit. Consequently, their ages will increase up to one hundred years. At that time, Jambūdvīpa will be full of men like a forest full of bamboo. Rich and prosperous villages, towns and cities will abound. All these wealthy kingdoms will be devoid of fear from robbers. Even the city of Baranas [Benares] will be known then.

Then the *kuśala dharma* will increase; the age of the people will also increase to ninety thousand years; the name of the city of Baranas will change to Uppala and will expand in size to one *yojana* in every direction. After the time when the age limit has increased to one hundred thousand, the city of Uppala will expand to seven *yojana*s in length and will become known as Paduma. After that, on account of continuously improving virtues, the age limit will increase to an asaṃkhyā. Then the name of the city of Paduma will change to Mandārā and expand its length to twelve *yojana*s. In that time, the human world will surpass even the heavens with regard to age. As it has been said:

> At that time, the country called Jambūdvīpa will be full of villages, towns and cities with many prosperous people, and it will surpass in age limits even the worlds of the gods.

And so, people will generally forget when they were born, nor will they know when they are about to die. They will experience neither old age or decay; nor will they suffer from illness. Without realizing the cause of happiness or suffering, people will not be interested in making acts of merit; consequently, their ages will gradually decrease to eighty thousand years; maidens of five hundred years will marry lads of the same age; the whole of Jambūdvīpa will have food in plenty, many useful goods, and all of the five types of comfort. Fortnightly at midnight, the rain will nurture the fertility of the earth. And by that time, the name of the city of Mandāra will be changed to the kingdom of Ketumatī. It will be twelve *yojana*s long and seven wide. As it has been said:

Then there will be a kingdom called Ketumatī twelve yojanas long and seven yojanas wide.

The Fabulous Palace of Mahāpanada and the Story of Saṅkha

Long ago there lived a father and a son whose profession was basket-weaving. With the timber of the Diṁbul [fig] tree, they performed the virtuous action of building a house for the residence of seven *pratyekabuddhas*. As a result,[6] the son came to enjoy all the luxuries of various heavens for a very long time and was eventually born into the world of human beings when the King Mahāpanada lived in a palace constructed with seven types of gems and which was twenty-five *yojanas* high. There he enjoyed dancing, music and songs performed by thousands of artists and musicians and reigned for an *asaṃkhyā* before returning to the world of the gods to enjoy more of the divine life. Eventually, he returned to the human world during the time of our Buddha [Gotama] in the city of Bhaḍḍiya and was known as Bhaḍḍiya Seṭṭhi. Enjoying great comforts for quite some time and listening to the *dharma* of our Buddha, he entered the *saṅgha* as a *bhikkhu* and finally attained *nirvāṇa*.

His father was reborn time and again throughout the vari-

---

6. The spectacular *karmic* consequence following this meritorious act is a motif frequently found in popular Buddhist literature. What it emphasizes is not so much the quality of the act *per se*, or the intention which gave rise to it, although these are important; rather, it reflects the importance of the quality of the object of the action (in this case, *pratyekabuddhas*). Furthermore, providing material support for the *saṅgha* and its members is popularly understood as even more *karmic*ally potent than actions of a moral nature. The rationale behind this understanding lies in the fact that the donor has contributed to the progress of another (in this case, a *pratyekabuddha*) whose destiny will be of a spectacular nature. Hence, the rewards for such actions are correspondingly spectacular.

ous heavenly abodes between the time of two buddhas. Because the merit of his deeds was more powerful [than his son's], he will be reborn into the kingdom of Ketumatī as the *cakravartin* named Saṅkha. [He will inherit] the palace of King Mahāpanada [his son], which is twenty-five yojanas high with one hundred stories and eighty-four thousand rooms made of gems. The first floor [will be] made of blue sapphires, the pillars of gold, the steps of silver and a golden roof with leopard figures will be made of corals. As a result of the king's giving of an *āvāsa* in a previous birth, this palace, made of seven types of gems, will lift up into the sky like a second moon and travel through the air illuminating the ten directions [before] descending to the center of the city. [In the palace of] seven types of gems, including the wheel gem, the elephant gem, the horse gem, and the gem of gems, his chief advisor, his wife and the eldest son, all things will be available to him. He will have one thousand sons equal to his strength. He will have the supranormal power of flying through the air; the fragrance of sandalwood will emanate from his body while the fragrance of water lilies emit from his mouth. Four deities bearing swords will stand guard at the four directions. The king's royal orchestra will cover an area of twelve *yojanas*, his *brahman* attendants will cover twenty-five *yojanas*, his council of ministers forty-eight, and the rest of his retinue will cover an area of ninety *yojanas*! His army, covering an area of five hundred *yojanas* will consist of warriors always dressed in uniforms made of the seven types of jewels. All around him, eighty-four thousand billions of his fourfold forces consisting of elephants, horses chariots will all be standing guard. Similarly, there will be eighty-four thousand kingdoms in Jambūdvīpa. In these kingdoms, there will be nine thousand million consecrated princes who will be attentive to that *cakravartin* Saṅkha. King Saṅkha will rule the entire world from that palace made of the seven types of gems. He will be attended by eighty-four thousand female dancers, like *apsaras* in appearance, experts in the four types of music, thoroughly feminine in grace and manner, and accomplished in the arts of glancing and smiling. While ruling the world thus, and accompanied by innumerable armies just like the full moon is surrounded by stars, in great royal splendor, travelling through the air[7] to all four continents surrounding Mahā Meru with their five hundred small islands, preaching *pañcaśīla* to all the people so that they do not cause demerit, will return to his palace for a banquet. As it has been said:

> That great King Saṅkha, possessor of many mighty forces, possessor of the seven great gems, a powerful *cakravartin*, capable of performing miracles, contented with every comfort, having conquered his enemies, will rule according to Dhamma.

Ketumatī: The City of Wonders

The kingdom of Ketumatī will have broad and narrow roads decorated with gold and silver flags, decorative pots, and banners. Shops and stalls lining the streets of the city will sell expensive merchandise such as gold, silver and precious stones, different types of perfumes and spices; one will not be able to imagine anything not available there. The city will abound with lakes and ponds full of clear, clean, fresh, cool water and with lotuses and lilies of many colours. Trees in full

---

7. Flying through the air is a power frequently atributed to reclusive Burmese lay Buddhist holy men known as *weikzas* associated with the cult of Maitreya in popular folk traditions. Such ascetics are also linked to the cult of immortality, which may derive from popular Taoist sources, and seek to sustain themselves until the time of Maitreya's appearance when they will be able to achieve a culminating *nirvāṇa*. The same power is associated with Gotama in several mythic traditions in both Sri Lanka and northern Thailand.

bloom will provide shade for many stone seats. The city will be radiant with gardens full of trees such as the mango, rose-apple, jackfruit, sandalwood, pine, and other exotic flowering and fruit-bearing trees. At that time, the lakes, ponds and gardens alone will be enough to make the people happy. As it has been said:

> In that city, the beautiful ponds, various trees in full bloom, the rocks, and the parks will cause the people to be happy at that time.

The kingdom of Ketumatī will be surrounded by seven concentric thick walls, [one of them] made of the seven types of gems springing up from the earth will be so illuminating that people will not know the difference between day or night. One of the walls will be made of solid gold, another of *lapis lazuli*, another of *masaragalla*. The wall made of the seven types of gems will stand ninety feet high in the middle of the other walls. The walls made of gold, silver and *lapis lazuli* will stand outside the great wall in heights gradually descending. In between the seven concentric walls, seven rows of palm trees twelve feet high and made of gold, silver, *lapis lazuli*, crystals, rubies, corals and gems of all sorts will appear. Each row of palm trees will be situated near its respective wall [gold palms near the gold wall, etc.]. At the four directions of Ketumatī, four gates having seven stories each and made of the seven types of gems will beautify [the entrances to] the city. In front of the four gates, four *kalpa vṛkṣa* will spring up from the earth bearing all kinds of valuables and goods. Even if all the inhabitants of Jambūdvīpa were to avail themselves of all their requirements of cloth and ornaments from only one of those trees, that tree would not run out of valuables even after eighty thousand years. At the center of the city there will appear a great hall made out of the seven types of gems. On the four sides of the hall there will be more *kalpa vṛkṣas*. Similarly, at the junctions and street corners of the city, a number of *kalpa vṛkṣas* of all kinds of gems will appear by the power of the gods who will always be ready to serve the people with all the comforts they need.

In that city of Ketumatī, not a single person will live in a hut made of wood and leaves. Everyone will live in palaces made of the seven types of gems. In all of Jambūdvīpa, no one will engage in cultivation, in trade or in any other profession; and no one will suffer from hunger. In suitable places of the earth, a self-generating rice paddy will appear which will bear pearl-like grains with a fragrance but no chaff. When the harvest of one of those plants is taken, sixteen *amunus* and eight *lās* of rice will remain after two thousand two hundred and seventy-two carts have been loaded! When this rice is cooked in a golden bowl on a hearth of gems on a fire rising from *jotirasa* [gems], everyone will consume it with tasty meats and other curries. When people feel the need to relieve themselves, a blue cloud will rush up to them and provide a cover. Instantly, a pit will appear in the ground. When they have answered nature's call, the pit will disappear and a pond of water will take its place. When they have washed in that pond, the cloud will disappear. Thus, the city of Ketumatī will be like a heaven. As it has been said:

> There will be a glorious city called Ketumatī inhabited by very rich people where there will be beautiful houses, pändals and gates which will shine like a heavenly city.

Jambūdvīpa: The Wonderland

At that time, Jambūdvīpa with all its [area of] ten thousand *yojanas* will be similar to the kingdom of Ketumatī, being as prosperous as a wedding house in season. In these kingdoms, men and women will wash and bathe in ponds with banks of white sands upon which stairs made of the seven types of gems lead down. These ponds will be frequented by swans and other birds and will always be covered by five types of water lilies. People will wear heavenly scents and creams, wreaths of divine flowers, selected ornaments and adorn themselves with garments and clothes given freely by the *kalpa vṛkṣas*. They will enjoy the taste of heavenly-scented rice, sit and lie on comfortable beds with heavenly bedspreads, sleep while listening to music and watch the dancing of artists who resemble the artists in heaven. They will awaken from sleep hearing music and see their wealth and comforts by the light of lamps burning with scented oil. They will be especially happy when they see their great wealth of cash, grains, elephants, horses, servants and laborers. As their minds will be full of happiness, they will enjoy this life full of luxury and comfort. None of them will suffer from the ninety-eight or ninety-nine types of illness nor from the two hundred and three accidents. Their bodies will be as healthy as the gods. As it has been said:

> The people of Jambūdvīpa will be rich and prosperous. They will always be happy and gay, peaceful in mind, enjoying the five types of comforts, adorning their bodies with various ornaments which, devoid of all ailments, will shine like the bodies of the gods.

Cakravartin Saṅkha's Meritorious Rewards

As a result of his giving an *āvāsa* made of Dimbul wood, this *cakravartin* Saṅkha will receive a great palace. Since he provided one bed, he will receive eighty-four thousand beds. For having donated one bed sheet, he will receive eighty-four thousand bed spreads; for the giving of alms which he had earned through hard labour, he will eat heavenly food; for giving one chair, he will have eighty-four thousand thrones. Because he observed *śīla*, he will be attended by eighty-four thousand queens; the chief queen will be the woman who cooked rice for the almsgiving with a pious mind. The merit-making act of erecting a fence around the *āvāsa* will be the cause of the seven great walls. The seven lines of palms will be the result of his having planted just one palm at the *āvāsa*. For his providing food and drink during the rain retreat season, the seven types of gems will appear. Because he provided cloth for new robes at the end of the rain retreat season, all the *kalpa vṛkṣas* will appear.[8] And so the *cakravartin* Saṅkha will enjoy these glorious comforts of a universal sovereign which resemble those of the *devarāja* Śakra.

Maitreya's Invitation to Buddhahood

At that time, when the human world is more comfortable than the heavens and when men will live for eighty-four thousand years, all the Śakras, Brahmās, Suyamas, Santuṣitas and Sunirmitas, all the *brahmās* and *devas* of the ten thousand universes which surround this fortunate galaxy[9] of ours, will gather and approach Bodhisattva Maitreya living in the Tuṣita heaven and invite him as follows:

> O Great Lord, now is the time for you to become a Buddha.
> Then, the great bodhisattva [will say]: 'Time, country, continent, family and mother; having observed these five, the buddhas will be born.'

---

8. *Cakravartin* Saṅkha's meritorious rewards in return for his pious deeds clearly depict the manner in which the doctrine of *karmic* retribution is portrayed in popular Buddhist literature and sermons. The layman's pious virtues are always begetting of cosmic reward if undertaken with the right intention and directed toward a powerful field of merit (especially the Buddha, *pratyekabuddhas*, and *arhants*).
9. 'Mangul-Sakvala': the 'good galaxy' because it is the only galaxy into which buddhas are born.

Bodhisattva Maitreya's Final Birth as Prince Ajita

Thus, having looked into these five great matters and having it confirmed by the devas that the time is right for him to become Buddha, he will be conceived in the womb of a *brahman* woman named Brahmawathie, the wife of the *brahman* Subrāhmaṇa, the chief advisor to the great king Saṅkha. Then after a lapse, he will be delivered from his mother's womb into the hands of Mahā Brahmā before a huge gathering of *brahmās* and *devas* of the ten thousand universes. With the appearance of his thirty-two marks, many miracles will occur and all the universes with mountains such as Cakravāla, Meru and Yugandhara will quake. Then growing day by day like the waxing moon and with all of the glory and prosperity of a child in heaven, he will become a young prince.

By means of the meritorious power of Bodhisattva Maitreya who will be named Prince Ajita, three palaces called Vardhamānaka, Siddhārthaka and Candra, made of the seven types of gems, will arise out of the earth and be his residences for the three seasons. Each palace will consist of seven stories and on each floor there will be millions of small rooms. Around each palace there will be seven walls of the seven types of gems. At the gates of the palaces will be *pandals* made of variegated gems. At the edge of the roofs of those palaces will be a golden mesh which will make music similar to that of the five types of instruments. On top of the palaces seven flags made of the seven types of gems will be hoisted. The whole city will vibrate with the continuous sound of golden chimes attached to the feet of the people. On the walls of the great palaces, decorative scenes of the following will be clearly visible: lines of palms, lions, elephants, coaches, peacocks, swans, curlews, storks, eagles, *garuḍas*, *nāgas*, *devas*, *brahmās*, creepers, trees, lakes, oceans, ships full of gold, silver and coral, Jambūdvīpa and other great islands, Ketumatī and other great cities, and other cloth paintings shining with the colors of the rainbow. Daily, showers of heavenly flowers will fall on top of those palaces. On every floor of those palaces, there will be seven thousand well-decorated chambers, seven thousand thrones made of the Vaidūrya gem, seven thousand parasols with handles made of gems and beds covered by multi-colored sheets. The pinnacles of the palaces will be made of gold. Around each palace, rows of elephants, numbering seven thousand in all, dressed up and attired with ornaments, will stand guard with their leader named Chaddanta. Seven thousand horses, whose leader will be Valāhaka,[10] will also be fully attired and waiting on guard. Seven thousand coaches shining like golden mountains will fly flags made of gems. On each floor, seven thousand dancing girls will await dressed up and ready to dance. The leader of the dancing girls will be Queen Candramukhī, who will be one of a kind, unsurpassed in her beauty. She will shine with the sixty-four feminine qualities. She will not be too tall, nor too short, nor too thin, nor too fat, nor too dark, nor too fair. In her exquisite beauty, she will be more divine than human. Sandalwood scent will issue from her body and the scent of water lilies from her mouth. The glow of her body will cover an area of twelve *riyan*. Her body will be as soft as well-cleaned cotton. She will have the five qualities of beauty: beauty of bones, beauty of muscles, beauty of complexion, beauty of hair and beauty of age. This will be her final rebirth[11]

---

10. Valāhaka is the mythic flying white horse referred to in the *Jātakas* and the *Karaṇḍavyūha Sūtra* who appears to rescue shipwrecked sailors from the island of the *rākṣasīs* (female demons who make their appearances seductive thereby entrapping their prey in lust before devouring them). In the *Jātakas*, Valahasa is the Bodhisattva Gotama in a previous birth; in the *Karaṇḍavyūha Sūtra*, it is the Bodhisattva Avalokiteśvara.
11. Ajita's queen is so exceptional that unlike other females, she will not have to become a nun (*bhikkhunī*) first and then be reborn as a monk (*bhikkhu*) to complete the spiritual path.

as she will have completed all the necessary merits to become an *arhant* and attain *nirvāṇa*. As it has been said:

> Having great amounts of merit earned over a vast period of time, being extremely beautiful, soft and gentle, having a pretty face like the moon, the wife of the bodhisattva will also be in her final birth.

The son of the *mahābodhisattva* will be named Prince Brahmavardhana and will be the oldest of one thousand sons.

In each palace there will be four pits of treasure one *yojana* in length, one *yojana* in width and one *yojana* in depth. At the four corners of the palace, four *kalpa vṛkṣa*s will arise up out of the ground and bear all kinds of clothes and ornaments. Mahābodhisattva Ajita, accompanied by a retinue of women wonderfully attired and replete with feminine grace, will enjoy the five types of worldly comforts for a period of one thousand years in each of these mansions according to the season. As it has been said:

> The residential mansions of that bodhisattva will have floors made of gems, walls decorated with paintings, garlands of scented flowers hanging here and there, and will be full of pretty maidens dancing and singing.

Because of the power of Bodhisattva Ajita, all the kings in the eighty-four thousand kingdoms of Jambūdvīpa led by the *cakravartin* Saṅkha together with multitudes of human and divine kings, will approach him and say: 'Lord, we have all come to serve you.'

The bodhisattva will reply: 'I have enormous numbers of attendants and followers here. You may all go back to your own palaces and rule your countries [from there].' And so he will allow the kings and gods to go back. About eighty million ministers who were formerly the bodhisattva's companions in heaven and now born into the various families of the city of Ketumatī will continuously surround him as his guards.

Ajita's Great Renunciation

The great bodhisattva, enjoying all comforts similar to heaven's will live a lay life for eighty thousand years until one day on his way to the royal park, the *devas* will create the figures of an old man, a sick man and finally a corpse. After seeing these three signs and becoming disillusioned with *saṃsāra*, he will give up the three-fold intoxications of being obsessed with youth, health and life. Upon seeing a fourth figure conjured up by the *devas*, the figure of a renouncer, he will decide to become a *bhikkhu*. Having engaged in sporting activities in the royal park and returning to the city on a road decorated by the *devas*, he will go up to the fourth floor of his mansion, enter his chamber brightly illuminated and scented by golden lamps and enjoy physical rest for seven days while engaging in *pradhānavīrya*. On the full moon day of *Vesak* when all buddhas attain buddhahood, and on the day when Queen Candramukhī delivered Prince Brahmavardhana, he will wish to set forth on the great renunciation. Instantly, all the gods of the ten thousand worlds of this universe will congregate. In all the eighty-four thousand kingdoms of Jambūdvīpa a mighty commotion will ensue as everyone will be saying: 'It is Prince Ajita's renunciation, today.'

Then King Saṅkha, followed by a large crowd of dancers and people, will go up the golden hall of the bodhisattva. And remaining various castes and social levels *(kṣatriyas*, *brāhmaṇas*, *vaiśyas*, and *śūdras*), males and female devotees and ordinary people from all countries and states will bring flowers, scents, flags, banners, umbrellas, banana leaves, pots, wreaths and so forth and gather around the palace. In the sky, innumerable gods will change themselves into tiny figures bearing scented flowers in their hands and will fill the whole space with sounds of '*sādhu*'[12] and divine music. The entire earth will be covered with precious stones, flowers and powders dropped by the gods and *brahmās* watching from Cakravate Mountain and other cosmic mountains. At the moment that the *mahābodhisattva* thinks of renunciation, his mansion with its seven walls and seven gates together with all the dancers and attendants will instantly lift off into the sky. By the power of the *bodhisattva* and the *cakravartin*, the rest of the assembly will also be lifted into the sky. Whoever wishes to renounce along with the *bodhisattva* will see each other in the air. Then the ten thousand *mahābrahmās* in their ten thousand *brahmā* worlds will bear ten thousand white parasols each three *yojanas* high over the head of the bodhisattva. In the same manner, ten thousand *Śakras* will come out blowing ten thousand conches one hundred and twenty riyan long. Ten thousand *Suyama* kings of gods will stand fanning the bodhisattva with ten thousand fans. Ten thousand *Santuṣita* kings of gods will fan ten thousand palmyra fans made of gems. Ten thousand musicians of the gods who are *pañcaśikha* will play the *vīṇā*. Forty thousand *varam* gods will guard the four directions bearing swords in their hands. Thirty-two male and female deities will bring heavenly scents, flowers and powders in caskets of gold and silver. A further eight thousand captains will protect the *bodhisattva* bearing swords in hands. Holding gold and silver flags, *asuras* will surround the *bodhisattva*. *Devanāgarājas* will bear torches made of gems. Divine garuḍas will gather to sing songs of praise. Human-like beings will also come to sing in their sweet voices. As it has been said:

Pretty *kinnaras* and *kinnara* maidens gathered in his

---

12. A swooning cry among the laity heard at the appearance of a Buddhist holy man or at the end of a sermon or ritual. Roughly, it means 'holy' or 'amen' and is an affirmative exclamation.

> garden will make him happy by fascinating performances of dance and song.

Furthermore, *apsaras* and *gandharvas* will throng from ten directions singing and dancing. Surrounded and followed by all these divine and human beings in such a festive mood, the air will be filled with the sounds of dancing mountains, leopards, *yakṣas*, the god's singing '*sādhu*', along with the praises of the *asuras* and applause from the *brahmās*.

The bodhisattva, having gone to his bodhi tree, will descend from the sky with his mansion. Mahābrahmā will bring him the eight requisites for monkhood. The *mahābodhisattva* will come down out of his mansion and cut off his hair with his golden sword, throw it up into the air, and receive the eight requisites. At the door of his palace, he will become a *bhikkhu*. On that day, eighty-four thousand *brahman* will follow the lead of the *bodhisattva* and become *bhikkhus*. At that time, two *brahman* brothers named Isidatta and Pūraṇa will become *bhikkhus* with eighty-four thousand followers. Two other *brahmans* named Hitamitra and Vijitamitra, capable of becoming *arhants* at hearing the first sermon will enter the order with eighty-four thousand followers each. A merchant by the name of Siddhārtha will enter the *saṅgha* with a company of layman numbering eighty-four thousand. A laywoman named Sudhanā will enter the order with eighty-four thousand followers. Two of her well-known friends, Yaśovatī and Viśākhā, who made much merit during the time of our buddha, will enter the order accompanied by their retinues of eighty-four thousand followers each. Large numbers of people belonging to the four castes living in and out of the city will become *bhikkhus* on that same day. As it has been said:

> Eighty-four thousand *brahmans*, all masters of the Vedas, will become *bhikkhus* following Metteyya.

The Battle with Māra—Lord of the Dead

This great *bodhisattva*, having made his renunciation, becoming a *bhikkhu* observing *śīla*, bathing in the river to cool his body, eating delicious milk-rice cooked in heavenly juices by his [former] queen Chandramukhī, sending his almsbowl upstream to the abode of the *nāgas*, sojourning for a day amidst festivities and offerings along a path prepared by attendant *devas* and *brahmās* from the ten thousand universes, taking eight handfuls of arrow grass offered by a devotee, will approach his *Nāga Śrī Bodhi* from the right side, circumambulate the tree three times in *pradakṣiṇā* fashion, examine the ground and spreading grass on that unconquerable spot, sit on the special seat of victory which will spontaneously spring up from the earth, place his back against the trunk of that *bodhi* [tree], and will await on that Diamond throne (*vajrāsana*) in four-fold determination. At that moment, Vasavarti Māra, living in his abode and knowing that the *bodhisattva* awaits in four-fold determination to become a buddha, will think thus: 'I will not allow him to become a buddha; I will throw him out of the universe taking him by his legs.'

Followed by his *māra* forces (the *Dasabimbaras*—who are ten times heavier than the earth) fierce and dangerous as they descend to the threshold of the universe, Māra will crane his neck to see but will fail even to approach Bodhisattva Maitreya, whose face is the symbol of compassion, and will beat a path backward in retreat. At this time, the sun, fifty *yojanas* in size, will shine its thousands of rays on the 'mountain of setting' like a great wheel being drowned in the ocean; meanwhile, the moon, forty-nine *yojanas* in size, will rise up out of the east as if to bathe the whole world in a milky ocean.

The Enlightenment

At this time, the great *bodhisattva*, awaiting under the *bodhi* tree, will illuminate the entire region around him with a golden halo emanating from his body. All the gods and *brahmās* of the ten thousand universes, having followed him during his renunciation and paying tributes by music and dance, will continue to sing his praises. The sky will fill with showers of heavenly fragrant flowers. Then that *mahāsattva*, taking up his Diamond throne under the *bodhi* tree, which itself is like a parasol made of emeralds, will sit in the hall of the universe illuminated by the golden light of the moon and surrounded like a curtain by the Cakravate mountains. Multitudes of gods and men will await in hopeful fashion. The great *bodhisattva* will then develop the special power of remembering past births during the first watch of the night; during the second watch, he will cultivate the power of seeing distant things; and in the last watch of the night while meditating on the twelve facets of *pratītyasamutpāda* in ascending and descending orders, he will gain omniscience and attain buddhahood just as the first rays of the morning sun appear.

Instantaneously, as on the day of his conception, the thirty-two auspicious signs will appear. The ten thousand universes will be adorned with earthly and divine flowers thickly and tightly arranged in wreaths on tables of floral design. That omniscient Maitreya, having attained all-perceiving wisdom making the entire world filled with celebration, will begin to express his exultation in words [after] spending seven weeks [in meditation on *dharma*] under the *bodhi* [tree].

Maitreya's Salvific Message

Pondering the depth of his *dharma* during the eighth week and accepting an invitation [to preach] by Mahā Brahmā, going into a grove of Nā trees called Isipatana[13] and sitting

13. The 'place where offerings are made to the *ṛṣis* (seers, ascetics)'; popularly known as 'Deer Park' and located in Sarnath near Benares where buddhas first preach.

amidst an assembly of human and divine beings covering over one hundred *yojanas*, the entire length and width of this universe, the Buddha will turn the wheel of dharma which consists of the four noble truths: the truth of unsatisfactoriness, the truth of the origin of unsatisfactoriness, the truth of the elimination of unsatisfactoriness, and the truth of the way to final emancipation. Then billions of human beings and countless multitudes of *devas* and *brahmās* will attain *nirvāṇa* by understanding the four truths and their fruits.

While Maitreya Buddha saves the world by preaching his *dharma*, the *cakravartin* Saṅkha will offer to Maitreya and his great *saṅgha* his royal palace covering twenty-five *yojanas*, give his enormous wealth to beggars and the poor and, approaching the Buddha with a vast retinue, worship him with utter devotion, listen to his *dharma*, cleanse his mind, attain *nirvāṇa* and enter the *saṅgha* with all his followers by Maitreya's simple inducement: 'Come, O *bhikkhu*.'[14] Then all of the gods and men will approach the Buddha and ask him questions regarding the four noble truths. The Buddha will respond in order to help them attain *nirvāṇa*. As a result, eighty thousand billions of men and gods will be saved from the ocean of *saṃsāra*. That ocean of *saṃsāra*, filled with the water of suffering with its waves of birth, old age and sickness, its whirlpools of desirous forms and sounds, its fish being like the various passion, residence of the female water-demons, is fed by the river waters of desire. Its length, width and depth

---

14. '*Ehi bhikkhu bhava*.' This is the phrase used repeatedly by Gotama in the early missionary phase of his life when converting new members to the *saṅgha*. In popular accounts, converts are instantaneously transformed in appearance with head shaved and dressed in the orange robe of a *bhikkhu*. In the early *Vinaya* accounts, all the Buddhas' initial converts are admitted by this simple yet miraculous means. But as the account continues, the authority to admit new members is delegated and a period of novitiate training is introduced.

can never be fully measured. Maitreya saves all beings sunk into the ocean of *saṃsāra* who are about to fall into the furnace of hell under the sea which is shaped liked the head of a mare.

The Ornament of the Saṅgha

Of the *bhikkhus* assisted by the Buddha to attain *nirvāṇa*, hundreds of thousands will always remain with him. All those *bhikkhus* will cultivate six *abhijñās* and ten *ṛddhis* and will be adept in the four-fold qualities [of an arhant]: *artha*, *dharma nirukti*, and *pratibhāṇa*. Having become well-versed in the *dharma* of the Buddha, having mastered all of it, they will be called *dharmadharas*. Accomplished in morality and very learned, they will be known over the entire world as the ornament of the *saṅgha*. Maitreya will be accompanied by this *saṅgha* of about one hundred million whose virtues will be innumerable. That buddha will be accompanied by a great *saṅgha*; just like Mt. Meru is surrounded by the seven Kula Parvatas; like a golden boat shining in a grove of fully bloomed lotuses; like a pillar of lamps shining amidst a multitude of other lamps; like the full moon shining amidst a cluster of bright stars; like a great sovereign accompanied by a great number of followers spreading over an area of thirty-six *yojanas*; like Śakra, king of the gods, among his divine following; the Mahā Brahmā in the company of *brahmās*; shining with the thirty-two marks of a *mahāpuruṣa* and the eighty secondary marks just like a lake of lotuses and other water lilies; like the sky illuminated by millions of constellations, like a golden mountain surrounded by rainbows and lightning making the whole world brilliantly lit with his glory and power. Decorating the whole world with the six types of colourful rays emanating from his body reaching all over the inner regions of Jambūdvīpa three hundred yojanas in length, all over the middle region which is six hundred *yojanas* in length, and over the greater region which is nine hundred yojanas in length, he will preach his *dharma* to the people helping them to earn the comforts of heaven and the attainment of *nirvāṇa*.[15]

The Great Offering and the Great Uproar

As Maitreya will be a powerful field of merit, people from all quarters will bring hundreds of cart-loads of food, drink, beds, carriages, cloths, perfumes, lamps and other requisites for almsgiving, but will have to wait nearby to get their chances. The sound of those cart wheels and the noise made by the waiting crowd will spread over a radius of thirty-six *yojanas*. There will be an enormous uproar created by those attending people, by the *devas*, *brahmās* and *nāgas* and by the *bhikkhus*, *bhikkhunīs* and their accompanying lay devotees. The sound will be increased by the hundreds of arriving carts, the praises sung by the *devas* and *brahmās*, and the beating of Mihingu drums by gods and men. Crowds of lined-up *brahmās* will arive holding white parasols and worshipping the Buddha. From another direction, throngs of devas wearing divine clothes will arrive casting bouquets of divine flowers, waving *camara* fans above their heads while making their offerings of dance, music and song. Retinues of thousand-headed *nāgas*, shining with jewels in their necks, will arrive offering forever-blooming flowers and then move backward placing their huge hoods

15. Whenever the Buddha is depicted as preaching to prospective converts in the early *Vinaya* texts, he gives two sermons. The first is about the power of meritorious and moral actions which lead to favorable rebirths in one of the heavens. If he ascertains that his listeners have gained the '*dhamma*-eye' (the ability to see things as they really are), he preaches a second sermon which consists of the four noble truths and noble eight-fold path leading to *nirvāṇa*. In summary, the two sermons represent the immediate spiritual aspirations of the laity and members of the monastic *saṅgha* respectively.

on the ground to worship the Buddha. Enormous *garuḍas* will fly behind the Buddha carrying large lotuses in their beaks. The Buddha will then receive these offerings from men, *devas* and *brahmās*. Amidst all these festivities, he will place his feet on large lotuses growing out of the earth on that spot. Or every step he takes, the ground will become even as all bumps and holes disappear. Gems of the seven types will appear where he has stepped. Even animals will be made happy. That is how he will come to receive his alms.

The Great Disciples of Maitreya

The *sāsana* of Maitreya will be known throughout the whole world. The entire Jambūdvīpa will be illuminated by the light of robes worn by *bhikkhus* and *bhikkhunīs* of his order. By the touch of breeze against the robes and bodies of the *bhikkhus* and *bhikkhunīs* visiting the houses of lay devotees, all sorts of diseases will disappear. On occasion, Maitreya will travel through the villages, towns, cities and states of Jambūdvīpa accompanied by his great disciples in order to coach the people on how to tread the just path. On occasion, he will cover great distance even to the heavens, the abode the *brahmās*, and to other universes past the edge of this one, appearing before those who have earned great merit in previous births and telling them how to attain *nirvāṇa*.

As stated in the *Nidāna Vagga*, his two chief disciples will be Aśoka and Brahmadeva and his two chief female disciples will be Padumā and Sumanā while his chief attendant will be Siṃha. His two chief laymen will be Sudhana and Saṅgha while his two chief laywomen will be Yasawathie and Saṅgha.

The Nāga Śrī Mahābodhi

The Nāga Śrī Mahābodhi under which Maitreya will sit during his enlightenment experience will be one hundred and twenty cubits in height. It will have five main branches of a similar length. From the roots to the top, it will be two hundred and forty *riyan* high. From the tip of the eastern branch to the tip of the western branch, it will be two hundred and forty *riyan* long. The circumference of the branches will be seven hundred and twenty *riyan*. It will look like a tightly gathered bundle of peacock feathers, or like a rock of blue sapphires shinning on top of a hill of silver beautifying the entire earth. There will be no gum or dried leaves falling from that tree. It will always be filled with dark blue and tender leaves like shoots of coral shimmering in the light breeze. Its flowers will be about a conch in size and in each flower there will be enough pollen to fill one small container. All flowers blooming on that buddha's day of enlightenment will last for eighty thousand years without withering. For about three surrounding *yojanas*, there will be many trees always inclined in the direction of the *bodhi* and always bearing flowers. On walls built of pearls and gems, creepers will surround the *bodhi* bearing variegated flowers in bouquets. One and a half *yojanas* around the *bodhi*, the ground will be covered with sand made of the seven types of gems. On the sand, water lilies will be strewn from the continuous shower of flowers falling. Five types of water lilies will be kept in many golden pots. Red lamps will line the gates. In the sky above the *bodhi*, canopies made of flowers with lotuses hanging from them will overhang. Even the birds will circumambulate the *bodhi* producing their sweet musical sounds and making offerings. No birds will perch or hide upon the branches of *the bodhi*. And so that great *bodhi* tree will shine in glory with all these beautiful qualities rivalling the beauty of the great parasol of Mahābrahmā. Men and deities will continuously approach and care for the tree with tender treatment and reverent offerings. *devas*, *brahmās*, *garuḍas* and *gandharvas* will never be satisfied as long as they gaze upon it. People from the various countries who come to the tree will enjoy the fragrance of flowers and powders that have been offered by the gods. Being so pleased, they will begin to dance and sing with praise. As it has been said:

> His Nāga Śrī Mahābodhi will always be full of flowers and fruit; its branches will be beautified with shining leaves. People from various states will approach the bodhi with incense and they will continuously make offerings of music, song and dance.

The Body of Maitreya

The body of Maitreya will be eighty-eight *riyan* high—from the feet of the knees, twenty-two *riyan*; from the knees to the navel, twenty-two *riyan*; from the navel to the cheekbone, twenty-two *riyan*; from the cheekbone to the top of the head, twenty-two *riyan*; and from the right shoulder to the left, about twenty-five *riyan*. His ear lobes, about seven *riyan* long, will be like two flashes of lightning. His eyebrows, five *riyan* long, will be like two blue rainbows appearing over a golden hill. His lips, about five *riyan* long, will be like creepers. His head will be twenty-five *riyan* in circumference as will be his face which will be like a golden mirror. His neck, like a Mihingu drum, will be seven *riyan* high. His round, soft and well-shaped arms will be about forty riyan long. His palms will be five cubits in length and each foot about thirteen *riyan*.

The sacred body of Maitreya will have two eyes which will be capable of staying wide open all night long, even in the pitch dark, and will be able to see tiny and large objects clearly for twelve *yojanas*. Maitreya Buddha's body will shine until the end of his life encircled by flames of glory that will reach for twenty-five *yojanas*. His body will also shine because of the thirty-two major and eighty minor marks of a *mahāpuruṣa*. It will shine like the sky illuminated by stars, like a great lake filled with lilies and lotuses, like a mine of precious stones and like a golden mountain covered by the evening clouds and lightning. The flames and rays emanating from Maitreya's body will be of six colors: like the rays of blue sapphires shining from a pot full of those gems; like the red rays of a pot of red coral; like the white rays from a pot of silver; like the variegated rays coming from a pot filled with seven types of gems. These rays will shine forth continuously, turning over and over, two by two, varying in size and filling the ten thousand solar systems beginning with the air-floor underneath beyond the end of the universe spreading across endless solar systems until the end of that buddha's *sāsana*.

Wherever Maitreya goes, lotuses will appear to receive his feet at every step. Of these flowers, the petals will be thirty *riyan* in size, smaller petals will be five *riyan*, buds will be twenty *riyan* and their sprouts will be sixteen *riyan*. Each flower will have buds of about one *amunu*. Whenever he steps upon these lotuses, the pollen will rise up to cover his entire body. White lotuses will appear between large red ones.

Maitreya's Miraculous Gandhakuṭī

All throughout the scented living chamber of the Buddha, *devas* and *nāgas* will create various types of lamps with a variety of gems. On the four sides of his chamber, there will be floral pandals and decorations. All will be eighty-eight cubits high. *Garuḍas* and *gandharvas* will decorate the ceiling and pandals with flags, chains of gold and silver, strings of pearls and gems and bouquets of fragrant flowers which will continuously shower. *Devas* will spray powders of scented sandalwood. Amidst the floral decorations, heavenly draperies of variegated colors will hang and light up the sky. Of all the floral pandals, those nearest to the door of the *gandhakuṭī* will be the most beautifully decorated. Between the two lines of pandals, there will be a special seat made of gems on which Maitreya will sit in the presence of his multitudinous disciples.

There, he will appear as if he were a *cakravartin* with a great force, like Mahābrahmā seated in the midst of *brahmās*, like Śakra (the *devarāja*) seated on the *Paṇḍu Kambala Śailāsana*, and like Mt. Meru surrounded by the seven *kula* mountains. There he will shine and make all people happy preaching his *dharma* so that they may attain *nirvāṇa*. At the four corners of his seat, there will be four bells thirty *riyan* high which will sound throughout the universe whenever they are blown by the breeze. This great hall of the Buddha, with all of its floral decorations and precious requisites and offerings, will follow the Buddha wherever he goes as if it were animated. The *devas*, *brahmās* and humans who witness this miracle will be overjoyed and seek refuge in the *triratna*. Sitting on that seat, the Buddha will preach his *dharma* so that the entire world will hear his voice. Due to the brilliance of that hall of gems, the light from all of the pandals, and the halo of six colors emanating from his body, the sun will not affect a difference between night and day. The light of the Buddha's body will spread over the entire world. During the age of Maitreya, people will only know the difference between night and day by hearing the crowing of the cocks and other birds in the morning and by seeing flowers in their morning or evening blooms.

That beautiful hall of gems will appear for the Buddha because of the power of his meritorious deeds. In that hall, there will be hundreds of gold and silver vessels filled with scented water and hundreds of urns made with four types of scent. In the four corners of the hall, there will be lamps made of jewels shining throughout the night. There will be lines and lines of urns and pots made of the seven types of gems and filled with bunches of red and white lotuses. On the roof of the hall, there will be lines of flags shining with gems of various colors. When the Buddha is invited to the house of a devotee, this wonderful hall will go along and settle in front of the devotee's house. Hearing the sounds of the bells in the hall, people will know in advance of the Buddha's arrival and will come forward to receive him. *Devas* and *nāgas* will also attend in disguise among the people and treat the Buddha to food and drink. As there will be no poor people in Jambūdvīpa at that time, all will gather to treat the Buddha and *saṅgha* with various kinds of delicious foods and sweets. The Buddha's preaching at the end of the almsgivings will be heard throughout the universe. All the people, staying in their homes and revelling in their joy about the Buddha, witnessing the glorious beauty of the great hall as well as the glory of the Buddha, abandoning [their former] faiths to take refuge in the *triratna*, observing *pañcaśīla*, living according to *brahmacarya*, cultivating the path and its fruits, and annihilating all of the passions, will reap the fruit of becoming an *arhant.* There will be no forest *bhikkhus* or any sects of *bhikkhus*. Everyone will engage in the ten types of meritorious acts such as giving and morality, will learn the whole of the *Tripiṭaka*, cultivate the path and its fruit, and by developing the order of the *saṅgha*, some will attain *nirvāṇa* in the present existence. Others will be born into the abodes of the gods and *brahmās* according to their respective attainments. At that time, everyone will make an attempt to listen to the noble *dharma* of the Buddha and gain *nirvāṇa*.

All the details and the description of this buddha and the precious and exotic things offered to him by the *devas*, *brahmās* and human beings cannot be described completely by anyone save an omniscient buddha himself.

Who Will See Maitreya?

In the time of Maitreya, all the people will live for eighty thousand years. Maitreya Buddha, who will live during this very period, will assist those who have gained merit during the lifetime of [Gotama] Buddha to ferry safely across the ocean of *saṃsāra* to attain *nirvāṇa*. His *dharma* and *sāsana* will last for one hundred and eighty thousand years.

Who are the beings who will see Maitreya and who will not?

Those who have committed the most heinous crimes such as killing one's father, killing one's mother, killing an *arhant*, harming the body of a buddha causing it to bleed, and causing schism in the *saṅgha* will be reborn in the Avīci hell and will not see Maitreya. Those who destroy *caityas*, cut down *bodhi* trees and ruin sacred images will not see the Buddha. Those who insult the *saṅgha*, spread malicious rumors about virtuous people and slander the *dharma* will not see the Buddha. Those who misappropriate gifts allocated for charity, those who abuse things belonging to the Buddha, *dharma* and *saṅgha* will certainly not see the Buddha. Those who wander with ash on the foreheads, who deny the present reality of existence, rebirth, actions and their consequences,[16] and deny the importance of father and mother, will not see the Buddha Maitreya. Also, those who have cursed the gods such as the sun, the moon, and the rain as well as noble people will not see the Buddha. Those born into the four hells, into the realms where there is only body and not consciousness, into the realm where there is only consciousness but no form, and those born into worlds outside of this universe will not see the Buddha. The disabled, the inhabitants of far away regions, monks of other religions such as the Jainas and the Ājīvakas will not see the Buddha.

During the age of the present Buddha [Gotama], those who engage in meritorious acts according to their individual

---

16. The references to those who wander with ashes on their foreheads and those who deny the efficacy of actions refer to *brahman*ical ascetics attempting to realize the true self of existence (the 'eternalist' position) and to ascetics who are fatalists believing that nothing can be accomplished through action (the 'annihilationist' position); these, then, are the great traditional philosophical extremes between which the 'middle way' is articulated. See *madhyama śraddhā* in the glossary.

capabilities will definitely see Maitreya. Those who observe *śīla*, give alms, build *caityas*, build temples and houses to eat, provide drinking water, help develop the Buddha *sāsana*, write and protect books of *dharma*, make preaching platforms, decorate sermon halls, offer scented flowers and powders, light lamps in the sermon halls, invite others to hear *dharma*, utter the word '*sādhu*' while listening to *dharma*, attend respectfully to those who preach *dharma*, organize *dharma* talks, support the writing of *dharma* books, all these will see the Buddha Maitreya and attain *nirvāṇa*. Further, those who provide alms to the *saṅgha*, who construct image houses, who paint eyes on buddha images, who nurse the sick, all these will see the Buddha. Those who have offered at least one flower, one lamp or even one spoonful of rice wishing to see that Buddha, and those wishing to share in the merit of those acts: all these will see the Buddha. Thus, all those beings who have performed meritorious works in previous lives will have the fortune of seeing the Buddha. Those incapable of attaining *nirvāṇa* will live happy rebirths in the six heavens and human world. Those who are born as animals will be able to attain *nirvāṇa* in their future rebirths.

Thus the Lord Buddha whose existence is in three phases at once—the past, the present and the future—satisfying the anxiety of the *devas* and humans, as one rain falls upon another, ended this sermon of the *Anāgatavaṃsa* and led large numbers of *devas* and *brahmās* into the sanctuary called *nirvāṇa*.

Benediction

May all people consider the results of the ten acts of merit one by one: purifying the three-fold motives, doing meritorious acts such as giving, morality, and meditation, sharing the merit of such acts with others while sharing in the joy of their meritorious acts [as well], preaching *dharma*, listening to *dharma*, attending and nursing the old and sick, purifying one's own mind with faith in the true *dharma*, treating elderly people with friendly words if they deserve such treatment. By fulfilling these ten-fold meritorious deeds, as a result of those actions, one will be reborn into one of the four castes in the kingdom called Ketumatī, will see the Buddha Maitreya, listen to his *dharma*, serve him with the four requisites, enjoy the three-fold comforts, and gain the final *nirvāṇa*. As it has been said:

> Leaving this life and reaching the city of Ketumatī,
> Being born there in a noble family,
> Going to see the Buddha Maitreya,
> May you possess the three-fold comforts.

GLOSSARY OF SANSKRIT, PĀLI AND SINHALA TERMS

abhijñā (Sanskrit)—degrees of 'higher knowledge' or 'insight' (supramundane in character) experienced in concentrated *dhyāna* (meditation) by a buddha or an *arhant* and leading to attainment of six paranormal powers: (1) seeing everything as it is; (2) understanding all discourse; (3) knowing the thoughts of others; (4) knowledge of one's own previous lives; (5) knowledge of the previous lives of others; and (6) the deliverance of the mind from conditioning and desire.

adhiṭṭhāna (Pāli)—self-determination, will, resolve; one of the requisite qualities for progress on the noble path of purity leading to religious perfection.

amuna (Sinhala)—a measurement used for determining amounts of grains or amounts of land needed to grow those amounts; an *amuna* of grain or rice is equivalent to approximately four bushels; an *amuna* of land is approximately two or two and a half acres.

apsarās (Sanskrit)—a class of heavenly dancers who are female divinities and wives of the *gandharvas* (singers and musicians in the heavens) capable of changing their shapes according to their desire.

arhanṭ (Pāli, Sanskrit)—an enlightened and enobled *bhikkhu* who has attained the end of the spiritual path culminating in *nirvāṇa*; a monk who, because of his spiritual attainment, is especially 'worthy' of receiving veneration from the laity.

artha (Sanskrit)—the skill of being able to completely look after one's own welfare.

āryaśrāvaka (Sanskrit)—a noble and faithful listener to *dharma* who aspires to live the spiritual life.

asankhyā (Sanskrit)—an incalculable number.

Aśoka (Sinhala form of Sanskrit and Pāli)—the great third century B.C. Maurya emporer of India whose reign is characteristic of a *dharmarāja*'s (according to traditional chronicles); remembered as 'Dharmāśoka', his life was so merit-filled from living by the truth (*dharma*) and promoting the welfare of Buddhism that he is popularly believed, along with the 2nd century B.C. Sri Lankan King Duṭṭha-gāmaṇī (Sinhala: Duṭugämuṇu) to become one of Maitreya's primary *bhikkhus*.

asura (Pāli)—a class of heavenly beings who do battle with the *devas*; they are uniquely celestial demons; birth into this class is one of the four unhappy destinies, but in this instance even they have been tamed in the presence of the *bodhisattvas*.

āvāsa (Pāli)—a monastic retreat or shelter, the provision of which by a lay person often generates meritorious and metaphysical reward.

Avīci (Pāli)—one of the great, miserable hells to be experienced by those who consciously and wilfully live a life of openly evil pretense and deed.

Baranas (Sinhala)—Sinhala for the great Indian city of Vārāṇasī (Benares) where in nearby 'Deer Park' (Isipatana) the Buddha set the 'wheel of *dharma*' in motion by preaching his first sermon.

bhikkhu (Pāli)—ordained mendicant of the Buddhist *saṅgha* living in the conscious practice of the *Vinaya* monastic disciplinary rules while studying *dharma* and cultivating the mind through meditation; as disciples of the Buddha's *dharma* who trace their spiritual lineage back ultimately to

Gotama, *bhikkhus* are often referred to as 'sons of the Buddha'; as such, they are venerated and patronized by the laity as 'fields of merit'.

bhikkhunī (Pāli)—the female order of monastic mendicants.

bodhi tree (Sanskrit, Pāli)—*ficus religiosus* (Sanskrit: *aśvattha*); the 'tree of enlightenment under which the Buddha attained supreme, supernal wisdom, vision and understanding of *dharma*; Maitreya's 'bodhi' is the Nā (Sinhala) or ironwood tree; it is also the National Tree of modern Sri Lanka; a sapling of the original bodhi tree at Bodha Gayā in India was brought to Anurādhāpura, the ancient capital and religious centre of Sri Lanka, by offspring of the great emporer Aśoka where it has thrived and has been continuously venerated since that time; while many miracles have been attributed to the power of the tree and it functions symbolically as an axis mundi in traditional Buddhist cosmology, its primary significance lies in its symbolism of the presence of the Buddha's *dharma*.

bodhisattva (Sanskrit)—an 'enlightened' and perfected 'being' on the threshold of *nirvāṇa* who continuously works for the supreme religious attainment of all and whose destiny as a buddha is assured; the initial use of the term in this text refers to the historical Gotama Buddha before his final rebirth.

brahmā (Pāli, Sanskrit)—a class of happily pure celestial divinities living in the heavenly abode of Mahābrahmā or Brahmadeva, the creator of the world; a very favorable rebirth.

brahmacarya (Sanskrit)—the living of a moral and chaste holy religious life as a way to end the experience of suffering.

Brahmadeva (Pāli, Sanskrit)—the creator god of the universe who initiates the beginning of a new *kalpa* (world temporal cycle) and at the propitious time invites the Buddha to turn the wheel of *dharma* by preaching his sermons of truth.

brāhmaṇa (Sanskrit)—a Hindu priest who officiates at ritual sacrifices, or serves as an advisor at the court of the king; the highest of the four *varṇas* ('castes') in traditional Indian society.

Buddhavaṃsa (Pāli)—'The Chronicle of the Buddhas' within which the prophecy of Maitreya is proclaimed succeeding the lineage of previous buddhas.

caitya (Sanskrit)—a domed-shape large scale reliquary venerated by Buddhist laity but within the boundaries of a monastic *vihāra* (temple) symbolizing the 'presence' of the Buddha, the path to *nirvāṇa*, and sacred cosmography.

cakravartin (Sanskrit)—the universal emperor preceding the appearance of the future Buddha who rules by 'turning the wheel' of *dharma* consisting of moral righteousness rather than physical force; legends surrounding the birth of Gotama assert that the infant possessed the thirty-two major marks and eighty minor marks of a *mahāpuruṣa* indicating his destiny to become either an enlightened buddha or a universal conqueror ruling according to the norms of *dharma*, i.e. a *cakravartin*.

Cariyāpiṭaka (Pāli)—the 'basket of actions perfected', the fifteenth book of the *Khuddaka Nikāya* within the *Suttapiṭaka* (collection of discourses of *dharma*) of the Theravāda Buddhist canon; the collection contains thirty-five *Jātakas* or 'birth stories' illustrating how Gotama successfully completed the ten perfections of the *bodhisattva* path.

dāna (Sanskrit, Pāli)—the culivated virtue of selfless 'giving'; cultically, the act of making an offering to the *saṅgha* and gaining merit *puṇya* in return; one of the ten spiritual perfections.

deva (Sanskrit, Pāli)—'a shining one'; a god or divine being within the heavens of *saṃsāra* who was formally a human being and will again be reborn as a human in order to attain *nirvāṇa*; the generic term for the higher gods of the pantheon.

devanāgarāja (Sanskrit, Pāli)—'the god who is the king of the *nāgas*' (serpent-deities of the terrestrial class).

devarāja (Sanskrit, Pāli)—'king of the gods', and epithet of Śakra (Indra) but also frequently used in referring to the exalted status of Buddhist kings (who are compared in might and splendor to Śakra.)

dharma (Sanskrit)—the truth of existence realized by the Buddha in his enlightenment experience; the teaching of the buddhas.

dharmadhara (Sanskrit)—reciters of the Buddha's teachings of truth, especially the 'basket of Sūtras.'

dhyāna (Sanskrit)—concentrated meditation calming and clarifying the mind and leading to insight into the true nature of existence.

gandhakuṭī (Sanskrit)—the 'flower-scented chamber' of a Buddha.

gandharva (Sanskrit)—divine beings of the heavens who are musicians and singers appearing at propitious moments such as the birth or enlightenment of a buddha.

garuḍa (Sanskrit)—the chief of the heavenly birds; Viṣṇu's vehicle.

Jambūdvīpa (Sanskrit)—'the island of rose-apple trees'; the central one of four continents surrounding the cosmic Mt. Meru; the human abode; India.

jotirasa (Pāli)—a wishing stone.

kalpa (Sanskrit, Pāli)—an enormous measure of time during which the world evolves and devolves signifying the continuous origination and destruction of world existence; a world cycle.

kalpa vṛkṣa (Sanskrit)—the heavenly wishing trees which appear during the first phases of a *kalpa* during the time of an enlightened buddha that provide for all human material wants.

kāmāvacara (Sanskrit)—the divine beings occupying the six heavens of the conditioned *sāṃsāric* world of desire: (1) *cāturmahārāja-kāyikas*, (2) *trāyastriṃśas*, (3) *tuṣitas*, (4) *yāma*, (5) *nirmāṇa-ratayas*, (6) *paranirmitavaśavartins*.

karuṇasāsana (Pāli)—'tradition of compassion'; referring to the Buddhist *saṅgha* in the widest sense as a community of compassion.

khanti (Pāli)—patience, forebearance; one of the ten spiritual perfections.

kinnara (Sanskrit)—a class of semi-divine beings with the figure of a human head and the body of a bird usually accompanying the *gandharvas* (musicians) and almost always associated with romance.

koṭi (Sanskrit)—ten millions.

kṣatriya (Sanskrit)—the warrior class, the second highest of the four *varṇas* (caste divisions) within traditional hierarchical Indian society.

Kula Parvata—the main mountain range in Jambūdvīpa.

kuśala (Sanskrit)—proper, prosperous, meritorious.

lā (Sinhala)—a measurement for rice and other grains equal to approximately one bushel.

Madhya Maṇḍala (Sanskrit)—the 'middle circle', the centre of the kingdom and Jambūdvīpa; the centre of the cosmos at the time of a buddha.

madhyama śraddhā (Sanskrit)—'middle faith or confidence'; the path of the Buddha is frequently referred to in Buddhist literature as the middle way between the extremes of eternalism (belief in a permanent self or soul, the affective counterpart of which is hedonism) and annihilationism (belief that the self is powerless, the affective counterpart of which is radical forms of asceticism).

Mahābrahmā (Sanskrit, Pāli)—Brahmadeva, the creator god.

Mahāmeru (Sanskrit, Pāli)—the mountain which is the *axis mundi* or pivot of this world being of immeasurable height at the top of which the six abodes of the gods are found;

surrounding Mahāmeru are seven mountain ranges separated by seven oceans.

mahāpuruṣa (Sanskrit)—'great person' born to become either a buddha or a *cakravartin*; in addition to size, the thirty-two major marks signifying his destiny include: *urnaroma* or white hair on the forehead, elongated ear lobes, fingers and webbed-toes of equal length, auspicious marks and patterns on the palms of the hands and soles of the feet, elongated arms, etc.; the size of the *mahāpuruṣa* indicates his cosmic status or his greatness; most sculptures of the buddha in his *parinirvāṇa* (reclining position) and many in his position of preaching (either sitting or standing) are enormous in size to convey his 'greatness'; the notion of a *mahāpuruṣa* has its origins in Vedic thought where the first being (*puruṣa*) is sacrificed by the gods in order to create the primary elements of the natural world and the social classes among men.

mahāsattva (Sanskrit, Pāli)—'great being', an epithet of *bodhisattvas*.

Māra (Sanskrit, Pāli)—death personified as a supernatural being who tempts humans to live according to the seduction of their passions thereby generating the types of actions which perpetuate continued suffering and rebirth in the conditioned existence of *saṃsāra*.

masaragalla (Sinhala)—a precious stone indigenous to Sri Lanka.

mettā (Pāli)— 'loving' kindness toward others; one of the spiritual perfections of the *bodhisattva* path.

mṛgasaṃvarṣa (Sanskrit, Pāli, Sinhala)—'rain of beasts'

Nāga Śrī Bodhi (Sanskrit)—the tree under which Maitreya will gain enlightenment; the ironwood tree, the national tree of Sri Lanka.

nā tree (Sinhala)—shortened form for *nāga*.

nāga (Sanskrit, Pāli)—a class of serpent divinities.

nekkhamma (Pāli)—patience, forebearance; one of the spiritual perfections.

Nidāna Vagga (Pāli)—the introductory portion of the text.

nirukti (Sanskrit)—uttered, pronounced, explained.

nirvāṇa (Sanskrit)—the extinguishing of the passions which give rise to actions fueling the cycle of suffering rebirths; the end of the Buddhist religious quest; the soteriological counterpart to the existential experience of enlightenment.

pañcaśikha (Sanskrit)—'five-crested'; the tufts of hair worn by an ascetic; the name of a divine musician in the *Dīgha Nikāya* who comes for counsel to the Buddha because he is love-sick.

pañcaśīla (Sanskrit)—the 'five-fold morality' basic to Buddhist ethics: abstaining from improper sexual conduct, taking life, false pretensions, taking what is not given, and intoxicants; rather than ruling by force, the *cakravartin* maintains order by promulgating moral actions.

pandal (Colloquial English)—a series of brightly decorated painted frames arranged in a circle depicting an exemplary event in the life of a Buddha or a well-known follower in popular traditions; in modern Sri Lanka, these large bamboo structures are erected on Vesak (the full moon day in May celebrating the birth, enlightenment and final *nirvāṇa* of Gotama Buddha) and Poson (the full moon day in June celebrating the coming of Buddhism to the island); they are now more than brightly decorated, for flashing light bulbs or neon tubes silhouetting each cartooned section create a major market place attraction at the time of these festivals; since these constructions are probably nineteenth century cultic innovations, the term here may refer to *toraṇas* (elaborate decorative architectural constructions over-hanging Buddha images symbolizing the world of *saṃsāra* by its representation of a collage of animals issuing from the mouth of Yama, the Lord of the Dead.

Paṇḍu Kambala Śailāsana (Pāli)—Indra's (Śakra-king of the gods) ornamented throne.

paññā (Pāli)—wisdom, insight, knowledge of all of the higher faculties of cognition; along with *śīla* (morality) and *samādhi* (concentration), one of the three elemental principles at the heart of the noble eightfold path leading to *nirvāṇa* and one of the spiritual perfections of the *bodhisattva*.

pāramitā (Sanskrit, Pāli)—the ten spiritual and moral perfections constitutive of the path of the *bodhisattva*.

pradakṣiṇā (Sanskrit)—a clockwise circumambulation of a sacred object (usually a *caitya* symbolizing the presence of a buddha).

pradhānavīrya (Sanskrit)—this is the great resolution of a *bodhisattva* not to leave his seat under the *bodhi* tree, even if his body suffers to the point of deterioration, he has gained enlightenment.

Pratyekabuddha (Sanskrit)—a 'lone buddha' or an *arhant* who is contented with achieving religious consummation in solitude.

pratibhāna (Sanskrit)—quick-witted, having the presence of mind or the ability to understand anything said or to say anything intelligently and eloquently; poetic intuition.

pratītyasamutpāda (Sanskrit)—'co-dependent arising', the twelve-fold cyclical process of causal conditioning affecting the perpetuation of *saṃsāric* existence which must be broken or transcended in order to make progress on the spiritual path to *nirvāṇa*; conditioning can be arrested only with the elimination or transcendence of desire or ignorance; the process which causes unsatisfactoriness (*dukkha*).

riyan (Sinhala)—a measurement of length approximately a cubit or one half of a yard.

sacca (Pāli)—real, truth, verily; one of the realizations to be perfected.

Śakra (Sanskrit)—name given by the Buddhists to the god

Indra, king of the *devas*.

samādhi (Sanskrit, Pāli)—concentrated meditation leading to ever-deeper experiences of equaniminous insight; one of the three basic practices underlying the noble eight-fold path leading to the attainment of *nirvāṇa*.

samāpatti (Pāli)—the meditative attainments including the awareness of the infinity of space, the infinity of consciousness, the reality of emptiness, and the reality of neither space nor consciousness.

samodhāna (Pāli)—collected, combined.

saṃsāra (Sanskrit, Pāli)—the conditioned, nominal existence of rebirths which is transcended when enlightenment and *nirvāṇa* are attained.

santuṣita (Sanskrit)—pleasure or content personified in the form of a deity or heaven.

seṭṭhi (Pāli)—a wealthy merchant.

śīla (Sanskrit)—morality, ethical behavior; one of the three fundamental principles upon which the noble eight-fold path is based and practised.

śūdra (Sanskrit)—the lowest of the four *varṇas* (divisions of castes) comprised of laborers in the service of the upper three.

sunirmita (Sanskrit)—the quality of 'well-constructed'; personified as a mythological deity bearing that name.

suyama (Sanskrit)—the quality of 'well-regulated'; personified as a mythological deity bearing that name.

thera (Pāli)—an 'elder' referring to a fully ordained bhikkhu (monk); 'theravāda' is the 'way of the elders' or the tradition of the Buddhist monasticism associated with the Mahāvihāra fraternity of monks in Anurādhāpura (the ancient capital of Sri Lanka) which became the normative orthodox tradition of Buddhism in Sri Lanka and Southeast Asia.

Tripiṭaka (Sanskrit)—the 'three-baskets' of Buddhist scriptures constitutive of the Buddha's canonical teachings:

Vinayapiṭaka (the scriptural traditions relating to monastic behavioral discipline), the *Sūtrapiṭaka* (the scriptural traditions containing his discourses on *dharma*) and the *Abhidharmapiṭaka* (the scriptural traditions relating to analyses of person, action, time, space, etc.).

Triratna (Sanskrit)—the 'triple gem' referring the Buddha, *dharma* and *saṅgha*.

Tuṣitapura (Pāli)—the 'city of satisfaction'; the heaven in the Buddhist cosmos into which *bodhisattvas* are reborn before their final rebirths wherein they achieve buddhahood.

Udaya Parvata (Sanskrit, Pāli)—the mythical morning mountain which catches the first rays of the day's sun.

upekkhā (Pāli)—equanimity; one of the virtues to be cultivated on the spiritual path.

vaiśya (Sanskrit)—the third of the four *varṇas* (caste divisions) comprised of farmers and merchants in traditional Indian society.

vajrāsana (Sanskrit)—'diamond-throne'; the seat of enlightenment under the bodhi tree.

varaṃ (Sanskrit, Pāli)—noble deities.

Veda (Sanskrit)— 'truth'; the body of ancient Indian scriptures mastered by brahman priests to effectively perform ritual sacrifices.

viriya (Pāli)—vigor, energy, effort; one of the qualities to be perfected on the spiritual path to enlightenment and *nirvāṇa*.

yamaka pratihārya (Sanskrit)—the miracle of making opposites (such as fire and water) appear at the same time; this miracle demonstrates the supramundane powers of the Buddha over the forces of nature.

yojana (Pāli, Sanskrit)—a measure of length approximately seven miles long.

INDEX

Abhijñās, 45, 57
Amitābha, 3
Anāgatavaṃsa Desanā
  as ritual text, 10-11
  literary character and history, 11
  cosmology within, 11
  social conditions of future in, 12
  doctrines in, 13-16
Apsarās, 31, 41, 57
Äsaḷa Perahëra, 9
Aśoka, 5-6, 25, 47, 58
Asuras 41, 58
Avalokiteśvara, 3, 10, 37n.

Bodhi tree, 42, 43, 47-49, 53, 59
  as *axis mundi*, 11-12
Brahmā, 24, 25, 36, 40, 43, 45, 51, 59
Buddhagoṣa, 8
Buddhavaṃsa, 21

Cakkavatti-sīhanāda-suttanta, 5
Cakravartin (*cakkavatti*), 21, 22, 23, 30, 34, 35, 51, 60
  ruling by *dharma* and *pañca-śīla*, 5-6
  and kingship, 7
  as Saṅka in *Anāgatavaṃsa Desanā*, 13
Cariyapiṭaka, 21
Cūḷavamsa, 6, 8

Daḷadā Māligāva, 9
Dhātusena, 6
Duṭṭhāgamaṇī, 6

Elāra, 6

Gandhakuṭī, 50-52, 61
Gandharvas 41, 50, 61
Garuḍas, 47, 50, 61

Jambūdvīpa, 23, 28, 32, 33-34, 38, 45, 61
Jātakas, 16, 37n.

Kalpa vṛkṣa, 12, 32, 33, 34, 35, 38, 61
Kāmāvacara, 26, 61-62
Karaṇḍavyūha, 37n.
Karma, 13-16
Kataragama, 9
Ketumatī, 25, 28, 30, 31-33, 55
  nature of Maitreya's future abode, 11-13
Kinnaras 40, 62
Kīrti Śrī Rājasiṃha, 9

Mahāmāyā, 21
Mahāpuruṣa, 13, 45, 49, 63
Mahāvaṃsa, 6, 16
Mahinda IV, 7
Maitreya, *passim*
  name in various Asian languages, 1; 22, n. 3

as symbol of Buddhist eschatological hopes, 1, 4
origins of cult of, 2-3
cult in China, 3-4
cult in Korea, 4
cult in Japan, 4
cult in Burma, 7-8
general Theravāda cult of, 4-6
king's as future realization of, 5-8
iconographic features of sculptures of, 8
as Nātha Deviyo, 9-10
as the *Cakravartin* Prabhavanta, 24
prophecy of buddhahood for, 23-25
as *Bhikkhu Ratna Sthavira*, 24
as Prince Ajita, 36-41
body of, 49-50
Mañjuśrī, 3
Māra, 21, 24, 42, 63
Mogallāna, 21
Mt. Meru, 11-12, 23, 51, 62
Mṛgasaṃvarṣa, 26, 27, 63
Muhurta, 23

Nāgas, 42, 50, 52, 63
Nātha Deviyo
as Maitreya, 9-10
Nirvāṇa, 13-16, 22, 31n., 44, 45, 46, 46n., 51, 54, 55
Nu, U., 7

Pañcaśīla, 5, 23, 31, 64
Parākramabāhu IV of Kurunegala, 5
Pāramitās, 21, 65
Pattinī, 9
Pratītyasamutāda, 43, 65

Ṛddhis, 45

Saddharmapuṇḍarīka, 3
Śakra, 24, 35, 40, 45, 51, 65-66
Saṃsāra, 23, 44, 45, 66
Sāriputta, 21, 22
Shōtoku, 4
Śuddhodana, 21

Tuṣitapura, 21, 67

Vajracchedikā, 3
Vinayapiṭaka, 46n.
Viṣṇu, 9
Visuddhimagga, 8
Weikza, 31
Yakṣas, 41

BUDDHIST TRADITION SERIES

General Editor: ERNST STEINKELLNER
Joint General Editor: ALEXANDER VON ROSPATT
Founder Editor: Late ALEX WAYMAN
ISBN: 978-81-208-0287-2

1 Indian Buddhism—*Hajime Nakamura*
2 Nagarjuniana—*Chr. Lindtner*
3 Chinese Monks in India—*Latika Lahiri*
4 Buddhism in Central Asia—*B.N. Puri*
5 Dharmakīrti's Theory of Hetu-Centricity of Anumāna—*M. R. Chinchore*
6 The Legend of King Aśoka—*John S. Strong*
7 Buddhist Insight—*George R. Elder*
8 Buddhism Transformed—*Richard Gombrich* and *Gananath Obeyesekere*
9 The Buddhist Tantras—*Alex Wayman*
10 The Lion's Roar of Queen Śrīmālā —*Alex Wayman* and *Hideko Wayman*
11 The Buddha Nature—*Brian E. Brown*
12 Evolution of Stupas in Burma —*Sujata Soni*
13 Buddhist Parables—*E. W. Burlingame*
14 The Debate of King Milinda —*Bhikkhu Pesala*
15 The Chinese Madhyama Āgama and the Pāli Majjhima Nikāya—*Bhikṣu Thich Minh Chau*
16 Sudden and Gradual—*Peter N. Gregory*
17 Yoga of the Guhyasamājatantra—*Alex Wayman*
18 The Enlightenment of Vairocana —*Alex Wayman* and *R. Tajima*
19 A History of Indian Buddhism—Tr. *Hirakawa Akira*, Ed. *Paul Groner*
20 Introduction to the Buddhist Tantric Systems—*F.D. Lessing* and *Alex Wayman*
21 Anāgatavaṃsa Desanā—Tr. *Udaya Meddegama*, Ed. *John Clifford Holt*
22 Chinnamastā—*Elisabeth Anne Benard*
23 On Voidness—*Fernando Tola* and *Carmen Dragonetti*
24 Nāgārjuna's Refutation of Logic (Nyāya) Vaidalyaprakaraṇa—*Fernando Tola* and *Carmen Dragonetti*
25 The Buddhist Art of Nāgārjunakoṇḍa —*Elizabeth Rosen Stone*
26 Discipline—*John C. Holt*
27 Philosophy and its Development in the Nikāyas and Abhidhamma —*Fumimaro Watanabe*
28 Untying the Knots in Buddhism —*Alex Wayman*
29 Early Buddhist Theory of Knowledge —*K. N. Jayatilleke*
30 Calming the Mind and Discerning the Real—Tr. *Alex Wayman*
31 A Comparative Study of the Prātimokṣa—*W. Pachow*
32 The Rise of Esoteric Buddhism in the Tibet—*Eva M. Dargyay*
33-35 Saṃyuktābhidharmahṛdaya (3 Parts) —*Bart Dessein*
36 A Millennium of Buddhist Logic —*Alex Wayman*
37 The Buddhist Pilgrimage—*Duncan Forbes*
38 Chanting the Names of Mañjuśrī —*Alex Wayman*
39 The Literature of the Personalists of Early Buddhism—*Bhikshu Thich Thien Chau*

40 The Laṅkāvatāra Sūtra—*D.T. Suzuki*

41 Studies in the Laṅkāvatāra Sūtra —*D.T. Suzuki*

42 The Vimalakīrti Sūtra—*Burton Watson*

43 The Gāndhārī Dharmapada—*John Brough*

44 Imaging Wisdom—*Jacob N. Kinnard*

45 Pain and Its Ending—*Carol S. Anderson*

46 Apparitions of the Self—*Janet Gyatso*

47-49 Rules for Nuns according to the Dharma-guptakavinaya (3 Parts) —*Ann Heirman*

50 The Chinese Hevajratantra—*Ch. Willemen*

51 The Historical Buddha—*H.W. Schumann*

52 Dana—*Ellison Banks Findly*

53 Hermeneutics & Tradition in the *Saṃdhinirmocana-sūtra*—*John Powers*

54 Skillful Means—*John W. Schroeder*

55 The Two Truths in Chinese Buddhism —*Chang-Qing Shih*

56 The Bodhisattva Path—*Jan Nattier*

57 Becoming the Buddha—*Donald K. Swearer*

58 Approaching the Land of Bliss —*Richard K. Payne & Kenneth K. Tanaka*

59 Indian Monastic Buddhism: Collected papers on Textual, Inscriptional and Archaeological Evidence— *Gregory Schopen*